MS-DOS® 6 Quick Reference

Que Quick Reference Series

SALLY NEUMAN

Publisher
Lloyd J. Short

Associate Publisher
Rick Ranucci

Title Manager
Walter R. Bruce, III

Acquisitions Editor
Sarah Browning

Product Director
Timothy S. Stanley

Production Editor
Heather Northrup

Editor
J. Christopher Nelson

Technical Editor
Robert Waring

Production Team
Claudia Bell, Laurie Casey, Brad Chinn, Brook
Farling, Bob LaRoche, Linda Seifert, Tina Trettin

TABLE OF CONTENTS

INTRODUCTION

M S-DOS 6 Quick Reference is a compilation of the most frequently used information from Que's best-selling DOS books. This book's compact, easy-to-use format enables you to find the information you need quickly.

MS-DOS 6 Quick Reference gives you essential information on MS-DOS commands, CONFIG.SYS subcommands, batch files, the DOS Editor, and error messages. Each part is arranged alphabetically.

Although MS-DOS 6 Quick Reference contains essential DOS information, this book isn't intended as a replacement for the comprehensive information presented in a full-size guide. You can supplement this quick reference with one of Que's complete DOS texts, such as Using MS-DOS 6, Special Edition.

Put essential information at your fingertips with the MS-DOS 6 Quick Reference—and the entire Que Quick Reference Series!

HINTS FOR USING THIS BOOK

As you read this book, keep the following conventions in mind:

If a notation appears in boldfaced blue uppercase letters, you must enter it. If a notation appears in *italicized* type, enter the notation only when appropriate. Words that appear in lowercase letters are variables. Make sure you substitute the appropriate disk drive letter or name, path name, file name, and so on for the lowercase variable notation.

If a notation appears with this symbol, the program, parameters, or switches are either new to MS-DOS Version 6.0 or have been enhanced from the previous version of MS-DOS.

Commands for which MS-DOS provides backward compatibilty, although they are obsolete in DOS 6, are included on a supplemental disk available from Microsoft and are updated so that you do not have to enter SETVER. The text indicates which commands are backwardly compatible.

You can type commands, as well as all parameters and switches typed with commands, in either uppercase or lowercase letters. The FIND command and the batch subcommands are exceptions to this rule because the case of the letters may be important.

Note that you must follow the file specification. You cannot use notation that does not appear in the file specification syntax. For example, the notation d:filename.ext indicates that path names are not allowed in the command.

In most cases, you can substitute a device name for a full file specification.

On-screen messages appear in a special typeface.

You can execute external commands and batch files that reside in different subdirectories just as program and batch files on different disks. This summary's syntax has a *c* added to the disk drive name and path. The notation is:

*dc:pathc*command_name

dc: is the name of the disk drive that holds the command, *pathc* is the directory path to the command, and **command_name** is the name of the program or batch file.

This notation is valid for batch files and external commands, which are disk-resident commands that are not an internal part of COMMAND.COM.

The following rules apply for external commands and batch files:

- If you do not specify a disk drive name for the command (*dc:*), MS-DOS searches for the command on the current disk drive.

- If you do not specify a path name (*pathc*), MS-DOS searches for the command in the current directory of the current disk (or the current directory of the specified disk drive).

- If you do not specify a drive and a path name, MS-DOS searches the current directory of the current disk for the command. If the command is not found, MS-DOS searches the path specified with the PATH command. If MS-DOS cannot find the command after searching the path, it displays the error message Bad command or file name, and the MS-DOS system prompt (usually A:> or C:>) appears.

MS-DOS 6 COMMAND REFERENCE

APPEND

(Set directory search order)   **External**

Instructs MS-DOS to search specified directories on specified disks if a nonprogram/nonbatch file is not found in the current directory.

Syntax

To attach APPEND to the DOS environment for the first time, and to enable APPEND to search the path for data files, use the following syntax:

*dc:pathc*APPEND /E /X:ON

To attach APPEND to the DOS environment for the first time, and to enable APPEND to search only the current directory for data files, use the following syntax:

*dc:pathc*APPEND /E /X:OFF

To establish or change the data file search path, use the following syntax:

dc:pathc\APPEND

d1:path1;d2:path2;d3:path3;...

To temporarily disable searching the path for data files, use the following syntax:

dc:pathc\APPEND /PATH:OFF

To see the search path, use the following syntax:

dc:pathc\APPEND

To cancel the appended search path, use the following syntax:

dc:pathc\APPEND ;

Note that a space is required between APPEND and ;.

d1:, *d2:*, and *d3:* are valid disk drive names; *path1*, *path2*, and *path3* are valid path names to the directories where you want MS-DOS to search for nonprogram and nonbatch files.

Switches

/E	Places the disk drive paths in the APPEND environment variable
/PATH:ON|OFF	Searches the path for data files when turned ON. When OFF, it searches only the current directory for data files.
/X:ON|OFF	Searches the path for data files when turned ON. When OFF, it searches only the current directory for data files.

Using APPEND with [drive:]path parameters a second or subsequent time replaces previous append settings.

ASSIGN

(Assign disk drive)   **External**

Reassigns one disk drive to another for a program
or a command. (See also **SUBST**.) MS-DOS 6.0
provides backward compatibility with this
command.

Syntax

To redirect drive activity, use the following syntax:

> *dc:pathc*ASSIGN d1=d2 ...

To view the current assignments, use the following
syntax:

> *dc:pathc*ASSIGN /STATUS

To clear the reassignment, use the following syntax:

> dc:pathc\\ASSIGN

d1 is the disk drive that the program or MS-DOS
normally uses. **d2** is the disk drive that you want the
program or DOS to use, instead of the usual drive.
The three periods (...) represent additional disk
drive assignments.

Examples

To reroute any activity for drive A to drive C, type
ASSIGN A=C or ASSIGN A:=C:. A space can appear
on either side of the equal sign.

To redirect any requests for activity for drives A
and B to drive C, type ASSIGN A=C B=C or ASSIGN
A:=C: B:=C:.

To display all drive assignments, type ASSIGN
/STATUS.

Typing ASSIGN clears any previous drive
reassignment.

ATTRIB

(Change/show file attributes)   **External**

Sets, clears, or displays a file's read-only, archive, system, or hidden attributes.

Syntax

To set a file's attributes, use the following syntax:

> *dc:pathc*\ATTRIB +R +A +S +H
> *d:path*\filename.ext /S

To clear a file's attributes, use the following syntax:

> *dc:pathc*\ATTRIB -R -A -S -H
> *d:path*\filename.ext /S

To display a file's attribute status, use the following syntax:

> *dc:pathc*\ATTRIB *d:path*\filename.ext /S

R is the read-only attribute, **A** is the archive attribute, **S** is the system file attribute, and **H** is the hidden attribute.

The + turns the attribute on so that the file becomes read-only, marked as created or changed, marked as a system file, or hidden. The – turns the attribute off so that you can write to the file, mark the file as not created or changed, mark the file as no longer being a system file, or remove the hidden attribute.

d: is the name of the disk drive that holds the files for which the attribute changes or is displayed. *path*\ is the path to the files for which the attribute changes or is displayed.

filename.ext is the name of the file for which the attribute changes or is displayed. You can use wild cards.

Switch

/S	Sets, clears, or displays the attributes of the specified files in the current directory and all subsequent subdirectories

BACKUP

(Back up floppy disks or hard disks)   **External**

Purpose

Backs up one or more files from a hard disk or a floppy disk onto a floppy disk or another hard disk. MS-DOS 6.0 provides backward compatibility with this command. (See **MSBACKUP**.)

Syntax

> *dc:pathc*\BACKUP d1:*path*\filename.ext d2:
> /S /M /A /F:size /D:date /T:time
> /L:d1:pathl\filenamel.ext

d1: is the name of the hard disk or floppy disk drive you want to back up. **d2:** is the hard disk or floppy disk drive that receives the backup files. *path*\ is the initial directory path for backup, if needed.

filename.ext is the name of the file(s) you want to back up. You can use wild cards.

Examples

To back up the entire hard disk, type
BACKUP C:\ A: /S.

To back up a single directory, type
BACKUP C:\DATA A:.

To back up a single file, type BACKUP C:*.LET A:.

To back up all files that were changed on or after Jan. 21, 1993, type BACKUP C:\ A: /S /D:1/21/93.

To back up all files in and below the \DATA directory that changed since the last backup procedure and append them to the end of the backup disks, type BACKUP C:\DATA A: /S /M /A.

CD or CHDIR

(Change directory)   **Internal**

Changes the current directory or shows the path of the current directory.

Syntax

To change the current directory, use the following syntax:

CHDIR *d:path*   or   CD *d:path*

To show the current directory path on a disk drive, use the following syntax:

CHDIR *d:*   or   CD *d:*

d: is a valid disk drive name, and **path** is a valid directory path.

Rules

If you do not indicate a disk drive, the current disk drive is used.

If you specify an invalid path, MS-DOS displays an error message and remains in the current directory.

Examples

To direct MS-DOS to move from the root directory to the directory named DOS, type CD DOS.

To direct MS-DOS to move from the root directory to HARDDISK, type CD DOS\HARDDISK.

To direct MS-DOS to move from the \DOS\HARDDISK directory to the DOS directory, type CHDIR .., CHDIR \DOS, CD .., or CD\DOS. No spaces appear between the two periods in CHDIR. MS-DOS moves from HARDDISK back to the DOS directory because the double periods represent the parent directory. DOS is the parent directory of HARDDISK.

(Change code page)   **Internal**

Displays or sets the code page (font) used by MS-DOS for all devices that display fonts.

Syntax

To change the current code page, type CHCP codepage.

To display the current code page, type CHCP.

codepage is a valid three-digit code page number. Valid codepage numbers are the following:

437	United States
850	Multilingual (Latin I)
852	Slavic (Latin II)
860	Portuguese
863	Canadian-French
865	Nordic

Note

This command requires that you load NLSFUNC.EXE as a device driver first.

CHKDSK

(Check disk)   **External**

Checks the directory and the file allocation table
(FAT) of the disk and reports disk and memory
status. CHKDSK also can repair errors in the directories or the FAT.

Syntax

*dc:pathc*CHKDSK *d:path\\filename.ext /F/V*

d: is the name of the disk drive you want analyzed.
path is the directory path to the files you want
analyzed. *filename.ext* is a valid MS-DOS file name.
You can use wild cards.

Switches

/F   Fixes the FAT and other
                        problems when errors are
                        found

/V   Shows CHKDSK's progress
                        and displays more detailed
                        information about the errors
                        the program finds. (This
                        switch is known as the
                        verbose switch.)

Examples

To instruct MS-DOS to analyze the hard disk or
floppy disk in the current drive, type CHKDSK.

To instruct MS-DOS to analyze the floppy disk in
drive A and ask permission to repair the FAT if a
flaw is found, type CHKDSK A: /F.

If MS-DOS finds an error, DOS may display the
following message:

xxxx lost clusters found in xxx chains

Convert lost chains to files (Y/N)?

If you press Y, CHKDSK converts the lost areas of the disk into files. These files appear in the root directory of the disk and use the name FILExxxx.CHK, in which xxxx is a consecutive number between 0000 and 9999. If these files do not contain useful information, you can delete them.

To instruct MS-DOS to invoke the verbose mode, which lists each directory and subdirectory on the disk and all files in the directories, type CHKDSK /V. Note that this output can be redirected to a file or printer.

To instruct MS-DOS to check whether all files in the current directory on the current drive are stored contiguously on the disk, type CHKDSK *.*.

The following message tells you that you are getting good disk performance:

All specified file(s) are contiguous

When the following message appears, the specified files are not stored contiguously on the disk:

d:path\filename.ext
Contains xxx noncontiguous blocks

This message appears for each file not stored contiguously. If you are analyzing a floppy disk and DOS lists many file names, COPY (not DISKCOPY) the files to another floppy disk. In the case of the hard disk, BACKUP your entire hard disk, reformat it, and then RESTORE the files.

CLS

(Clear screen)   **Internal**

Erases or clears the display screen.

Syntax

CLS

Rules

After clearing all on-screen information, MS-DOS places the cursor at the home position (upper left corner).

This command affects only the active video display.

If you use ANSI control codes to set the foreground and background color settings, the settings remain in effect. If you do not set the foreground and background colors, the screen reverts to light characters on a dark background.

CLS only affects the screen, not memory.

COMMAND

(Invoke secondary command processor)   External

Invokes another copy of COMMAND.COM, the command processor.

Syntax

dc:pathc\COMMAND *comspec cttydevice*
/C string /E:nnnn /K:filename /P /MSG

comspec is the path where COMMAND.COM is located. *cttydevice* is the device MS-DOS uses for input and output. The default is CON (the keyboard and screen).

Switches

/C string   Passes the string speci-
                   fied to the new copy of
                   COMMAND.COM, and then

	returns you to the original copy of the interpreter. The *string* is a set of characters such as a command.
/E:nnnn	Sets the size of the environment. Size(*nnnn*) is a decimal number from 160 to 32,768 bytes, rounded up to the nearest multiple of 16. The default is 256.
*/K:*filename	Runs the program you specify and returns you to the DOS prompt (not for use in CONFIG.SYS)
/MSG	Loads all error messages into memory. You must use this switch with /P.
/P	Keeps this copy permanently in memory (until the next system reset)

COMP

(Compare files)   External

Compares two files to see whether they are the same. MS-DOS 6.0 provides backward compatibility with this command. (See also **FC**.)

Syntax

*dc:pathc*COMP d1:path1\\filename1.ext1
d2:path2\\filename2.ext2

path1**is the path to the first file. **filename1.ext1 is the filename for the first file.**path2** is the path to the second file. **filename2.ext2** is the file name for the second file. You can use wild cards.

Also, **d1** and **d2** may be the same, **path1** and
path2** may be the same, and **filename1.ext1 and
filename2.ext2 may be the same.

Terms

d1:path1\filename1.ext1 is the *primary file name*.

d2:path2\filename2.ext2 is the *secondary file name*.

Switches

/A	Displays the actual differing characters
/C	Ignores case in the files to be compared
/D	Displays the hexadecimal values of the differing characters (default)
/L	Displays the line number of the differing characters found
/N:line	Compares the number of lines in a file. *line* is the number of lines to compare.

Rules

If you do not specify a drive name or path name for
a file, DOS uses the current disk drive and directory.
(This rule applies to *d1:path1* and *d2:path2*, as well
as to *dc:pathc*, the drive holding the command
itself.)

If you do not enter a file name, all files (primary
or secondary) are compared (which is the same as
entering *.*). However, only the secondary files with
matching names are compared.

If you do not enter a drive name, path name, and file
name, COMP prompts you for the primary and
secondary files and switches to compare.

If you are comparing files on floppy disks, the correct floppy disks must be in the correct drive. COMP does not wait for you to insert floppy disks if you give both primary and secondary file names.

COMP does not check files with matching names but different lengths. COMP displays a message indicating that these files are different.

After 10 mismatches (unequal comparisons) between the contents of two compared files, COMP ends the comparison between the two files and aborts.

Notes

If you have a program that once functioned properly, but now acts strangely, check a good backup copy of the file against the copy you are using. If COMP finds differences, copy the good program to the disk you are using.

If you are comparing ASCII files, you may find the /A and /C switches useful. These switches display the actual character differences and do not compare character case. If you are comparing binary files, you may prefer the /D switch to display differences using hexadecimal values rather than decimal values.

To find the last revision of a file, look at its date and time stamp in the directory to identify the most recent version. If you want to compare floppy disks that have been copied with DISKCOPY, use DISKCOMP instead of COMP.

COPY

(Copy files)   **Internal**

Copies files between disk drives or devices, either keeping the same file name or changing it. COPY can concatenate (join) two or more files into another file or append one or more files to another file. Options in this command support special handling of text files and verification of the copying process.

Syntax

To copy a file, use the following syntax:

> COPY /A/B d1:path1\filename1.ext1/A/B
> d0:path2/filename0.ext0 /A/B/V

or

> COPY /A/B d1:path1\filename1.ext1/A/B/V

To join several files into one file, use the following syntax:

> COPY /A/B d1:path1\filename1.ext1/A/B +
> d2:path2\filename2.ext2/A/B +...

d1:, *d2:*, and *d0:* are valid disk drive names. *path1*, *path2*, and *path0* are valid path names.

filename1.*ext1*, **filename2**.*ext2*, and **filename0**.*ext0* are valid file names. You can use wild cards. The three periods represent additional files in the form *dx:pathx/***filenamex**.*extx*.

Terms

The file from which you are copying is the *source file*. The names containing **1** and **2** are the source files.

The file to which you are copying is the *destination file*. It is represented by a **0**.

Switches

/V	Verifies that the copy has been recorded correctly.

The following switches have different effects for the source file and the destination file. Source file effects are as follows:

/A	Treats the file as an ASCII (text) file. The command copies all the information in the file up to, but not including, the end-of-file marker (Ctrl-Z). Anything after the end-of-file marker is ignored.
/B	Copies the entire file as if it were a program file. Any end-of-file markers (Ctrl-Z) are treated as normal characters, and the EOF characters are copied.

Destination file effects are as follows:

/A	Adds an end-of-file marker (Ctrl-Z) to the end of the ASCII text file after it is copied.
/B	Does not add the end-of-file marker to this binary file.

CTTY

(Change console) **Internal**

Changes the standard input and output device to an auxiliary console, or changes the input and output device back from an auxiliary console to the keyboard and video display.

Syntax

CTTY device

device is the name of the device you want to use as the new standard input and output device. This name must be a valid MS-DOS device name. Valid device names are as follows:

PRN, LPT1, LPT2, LPT3, CON, AUX, COM1,
COM2, COM3, COM4

Rules

The device should be a character-oriented device
capable of both input and output.

Programs designed to work with the video display's
control codes may not function properly when
redirected.

Examples

To make the device attached to COM1 the new
console, type CTTY COM1.

The peripheral connected to COM1 must be a
terminal or a teleprinter (printer with a keyboard).
After you issue this command, MS-DOS expects
normal input to come from COM1 and sends anything for the video display to COM1.

To make the keyboard and video display the
console, thus cancelling the previous CTTY, type
CTTY CON:.

Note

With the CTTY command, you can use a terminal or
teleprinter, instead of the computer's keyboard and
video display, for console input and output.

DATE

(Set/show date)   **Internal**

Displays and/or changes the system date.

Syntax

DATE date_string

date_string is in one of the following forms:

- ▦ mm-dd-yy or mm-dd-yyyy for North America
- ▦ dd-mm-yy or dd-mm-yyyy for Europe
- ▦ yy-mm-dd or yyyy-mm-dd for the Far East

mm is a one- or two-digit number for the month
(1 to 12). *dd* is a one- or two-digit number for the
day (1 to 31). *yy* is a one- or two-digit number for
the year (80 to 99). The first two digits of the year
are assumed. *yyyy* is a four-digit number for the year
(1980 to 2099).

Note

You can use hyphens, periods, or slashes as the
delimiters between the day, month, and year. The
displayed result varies depending on the country
code set in the CONFIG.SYS file.

 **DBLSPACE**

(Disk compression utility)   **External**

Compresses files on a disk drive in order to provide
more hard disk storage capacity.

Syntax

To use DBLSPACE as a device driver, use the
following syntax:

    DEVICE=dc:pathc\DBLSPACE.SYS

To use DBLSPACE as a command, use the following
syntax:

    dc:pathc\DBLSPACE /AUTOMOUNT /CHKDSK
    /COMPRESS /CREATE /DEFRAGMENT /DELETE
    /FORMAT /INFO /LIST /MOUNT /MOVE /RATIO
    /SIZE /UNMOUNT

Switches

/AUTOMOUNT	Automatically mounts a compressed drive
/CHKDSK	Checks the directory and the file allocation table (FAT) of the disk and reports on the status of the compressed drive's file structure
/COMPRESS	Begins compressing a hard disk drive or floppy disk
/CREATE	Using free space available on an existing disk drive, creates a new compressed volume
/DEFRAGMENT	Defragments files on a compressed volume to optimize the volume's performance
/DELETE	Removes a compressed drive
/FORMAT	Prepares a compressed volume to hold files and data
/INFO	Shows detailed information about a compressed volume
/LIST	Shows a listing of all compressed volumes and uncompressed drives currently installed, including RAM drives and floppy disk drives
/MOUNT	Mounts a compressed volume to access files on the volume
/MOVE	Loads the DBLSPACE.SYS driver with Quarterdeck QEMM's LOADHI.SYS program
/RATIO	Shows the compressed file ratio on a compressed volume
/SIZE	Adjusts the size of a compressed volume
/UNMOUNT	Dismounts a compressed volume

Notes

You must compress a disk drive by running DBLSPACE.EXE before you can use the DBLSPACE.SYS device driver. After you compress the disk drive, MS-DOS updates your CONFIG.SYS file to include the driver.

The default cluster size for DBLSPACE compressed volumes is 8K. The maximum size of a DBLSPACE volume is 512M.

DEBUG

(Run, Test, Edit Programs) External

Enables you to run, test, and edit programs.

Syntax

*dc:pathc*DEBUG *de:pathe\\filename.exte*

de:pathe is the disk drive and directory that hold the file you want to edit. *filename.exte* is the file you want to load into memory and edit.

DECOMP

(File decompression utility) External

Decompresses program files from the DOS distribution floppy disks. (See also **EXPAND**.)

Syntax

*dc:pathc*DECOMP *d:path\\filename*
d:path\\filename destination -F -Q

d:path\\filename is the drive, path, and file name of the file to be decompressed and the drive, path, and file name of the file DECOMP will decompress onto your hard disk. You can use wild cards.

Switches

-F	Instructs DECOMP to over-write the existing file, if any
-Q	Instructs DECOMP to calculate the amount of space the compressed file will be when fully decompressed

Note

If you type DECOMP without specifying file names, DECOMP asks you for the location and name of the file you want to decompress. Then, DECOMP asks you how you want to name the decompressed file and where you want DECOMP to place it. If you don't specify a destination directory for a new decompressed file, DECOMP uses the current directory.

DEFRAG

(Defragment files utility)   **External**

Defragments files on disks to optimize your disk's performance.

Syntax

DEFRAG d: /F /S:order /V /B /SKIPHIGH /GØ

or

DEFRAG d: /U /V /B /SKIPHIGH /GØ

d: is the name of the drive you want to defragment.

Switches

/B	Instructs DEFRAG to reboot your computer after all files have been optimized. Use this switch if you load FASTOPEN in your AUTOEXEC.BAT file
/F	Defragments all files so that no empty spaces between files remain
/GØ	Starts DEFRAG without graphics
/S	Specifies how DEFRAG is to sort files within directories. Valid sort order switches are as follows:

N	Alphabetical order by file name
N-	Reverse alphabetical order by file name
E	Alphabetical order by extension
E-	Reverse alphabetical order by extension
D	Chronological order, earliest date first
D-	Reverse chronological order, latest date first
S	By file size, smallest files first
S-	By file size, largest files first

/SKIPHIGH	Tells DEFRAG to load into conventional rather than upper memory (if upper memory is available)
/U	Defragments all files on the specified disk, leaving any empty spaces between files if

space existed prior to optimization

/V   Verifies that all files have been correctly written to your disk. Verification slows down the defragmentation process.

Rules

You cannot use DEFRAG on network drives nor on drives created with the MS-DOS utility **INTERLNK**.

Do not use DEFRAG inside Microsoft Windows.

DEL (ERASE)

(Delete files)   **Internal**

Deletes files from the disk. DEL is an alternative command for ERASE and performs the same functions.

Syntax

DEL *d:path\filename.ext* /P

or

ERASE *d:path\filename.ext* /P

d: is the name of the disk drive that holds the file or files you want erased. *path* is the directory of the file or files you want erased.

filename.ext is the name of the file or files you want erased. You can use wild cards.

Switch

/P   Instructs DOS to prompt you for delete confirmation.

DELOLDOS

(Remove Old DOS Files)   External

Removes old DOS files from the hard disk. MS-DOS 6.0 provides backward compatibility with this command.

Syntax

> dc:pathc\DELOLDOS /B

Switch

/B   Starts DELOLDOS in black-and-white mode.

Note

When you upgrade an existing system to DOS 5, the old version of DOS is preserved. Use this command to delete the old version of DOS.

DELTREE

(Delete subdirectory and all files inside)   External

Deletes a directory, and any and all files and subdirectories in the named directory.

Syntax

> DELTREE /Y dc:pathc\

Switch

/Y   Instructs DELTREE not to prompt you for confirmation before carrying out the command

DIR

(Directory)   **Internal**

Lists any or all files and subdirectories in a disk's directory.

The DIR command displays the disk volume name (if any), the disk volume serial number, the name of the directory (its complete path), the name of each disk file or subdirectory, the number of files, the amount, in bytes, of displayed files, the amount, in bytes, of free space on the disk, and, unless otherwise directed, the number of bytes that each file occupies and the date/time of the file's creation/ last update.

Syntax

DIR *d:path\filename.ext /P /W /A:attrib /O:order*

/S /B /L /C

d: is the drive holding the disk you want to examine. *path* is the path to the directory you want to examine.

filename.ext is a valid file name. You can use wild cards.

Switches

/A:attrib	Displays only those files that have the attribute that you specify. The settings for *attrib* are given in the following table.
	(/A only) Displays all directory entries, even system and hidden files

	h	Displays hidden files
	-h	Displays files that are not hidden
	s	Displays system files
	-s	Displays files that are not system files
	d	Displays subdirectories
	-d	Displays only files (no subdirectory names)
	a	Displays files for archiving
	-a	Displays files that have been archived
	r	Displays read-only files
	-r	Displays files that can be read and written to
/B		Lists only the root name and extension. This switch doesn't list any other information, such as size, date, and time created.
/C		Displays file compression statistics on DBLSPACE volumes. This switch does not work with /W and /B switches.
L		Lists file names and subdirectory names in lowercase
/O:sort		Displays the directory in sorted order. The following table gives settings for *sort*:

	(*/O only*)	Sorts directory entries alphabetically, listing subdirectories before files (0-9, A-Z)
	n	Sorts alphabetically by root name (0-9, A-Z)
	-n	Sorts reverse-alphabetically by root name (Z-A, 9-0)
	e	Sorts alphabetically by extension (0-9, A-Z)
	-e	Sorts reverse-alphabetically by extension (Z-A, 9-0)
	d	Sorts by date and time, earliest to latest
	-d	Sorts by date and time, latest to earliest.
	s	Sorts by size, smallest to largest
	-s	Sorts by size, largest to smallest
	g	Lists subdirectories before files
	-g	Lists subdirectories after files
/P		Pauses when the screen is full and waits for you to press any key
/S		Lists all files in the current directory and all subsequent directories

/W   Gives a wide (80-column)
                            display of the names of the
                            files. This switch does not
                            display the information about
                            file size, date, and time.

Notes

The DIR command finds the disk files or subdirectories on the disk. Unless you use the /S
switch, this command shows only the files and
subdirectories in the specified or the default
directory.

Using the /A switch, you may list only those files
with certain attributes. Listing files that can be
archived enables you to determine which archived
files you can back up or XCOPY. You also can sort
files in many different ways, which enables you to
better manage your files.

DISKCOMP

(Compare floppy disks)   **External**

Compares two floppy disks on a track-for-track,
sector-for-sector basis to see whether their contents are identical. MS-DOS 6.0 provides backward
compatibility with this command. (See also **FC**.)

Syntax

*dc:pathc*DISKCOMP *d1: d2: /1 /8*

d1: and *d2:* are the disk drives that hold the floppy
disks you want to compare. These drives may be the
same or different.

Switches

/1   Compares only the first side of the floppy disk, even if the floppy disk or disk drive is double-sided.

/8   Compares only eight sectors per track, even if the first floppy disk has a different number of sectors per track.

Rules

If you do not specify a drive name, DISKCOMP uses the first floppy disk drive (usually drive A).

If you specify only one valid floppy disk drive name, DISKCOMP uses that drive for the comparison.

Giving the same valid floppy disk drive name twice is the same as specifying only one disk drive name.

If you specify a valid hard disk drive name or invalid disk drive name, MS-DOS displays an error message and does not perform the comparison.

When you are using one disk drive, MS-DOS prompts you to change floppy disks.

You should compare only compatible floppy disks. The two floppy disks must be formatted with the same number of tracks, sectors, and sides.

Do not use DISKCOMP with an ASSIGNed disk drive. DISKCOMP ignores the effects of the ASSIGN.

Do not use a JOINed disk, a SUBSTituted disk, a virtual (RAM) disk, or networked disk drives with DISKCOMP. MS-DOS displays an error message.

Example

To compare the floppy disk in drive A with the floppy disk in drive B, type DISKCOMP A: B:.

DISKCOPY

(Copy entire floppy disk)   External

Copies the entire contents of one floppy disk to
another floppy disk on a track-for-track basis.
DISKCOPY works with floppy disks only.

Syntax

> *dc:pathc*DISKCOPY *d1: d2: /1/ V*

d1: is the floppy disk drive that holds the source
disk. *d2:* is the floppy disk drive that holds the target
disk.

Switches

/1	Copies only the first side of the floppy disk.
/V	Verifies each track after it has been copied.

Terms

The floppy disk from which you are copying is the
source or *first* floppy disk.

The floppy disk to which you are copying is the
target or *second* floppy disk.

DOSHELP

(DOS On-line Help)   External

Provides an on-line help summary for basic DOS
commands and syntax. MS-DOS provides backward
compatibility with this command. (See also **HELP**.)

Syntax

DOSHELP *command*

or

command /?

command specifies the particular command you want to see help about. Typing DOSHELP without any command displays an alphabetical list of commands for which summary on-line help is available.

DOSKEY

(Review command line/Create macros)   **External**

Remembers a history of commands typed from the command line for reuse or editing. You also can use DOSKEY macros to create custom DOS commands.

Syntax

dc:pathc\DOSKEY /REINSTALL /BUFSIZE=*bytes* /MACROS /HISTORY /INSERT *or* |OVERSTRIKE *macroname=macrotext*

macroname is the name assigned to the command or commands you want to perform. *macrotext* is the command or commands that MS-DOS performs when you type the *macroname* and press Enter.

Switches

/BUFSIZE=*bytes*   Sets aside memory for DOSKEY to store commands and macros. The value of *bytes* is the actual amount of memory to set aside. The default is 1024 bytes, or 1K bytes

/HISTORY	Lists all commands stored in memory from earliest to latest
/INSERT or */OVERSTRIKE*	Enables Insert mode or Overstrike mode. With Insert mode, you can insert characters when editing a command line
/MACROS	Lists all the macros created with DOSKEY
/REINSTALL	Reinstalls DOSKEY

Notes

With DOSKEY, memory stores a history of commands. The number of commands that memory
retains depends on the buffer size, which is, by
default, 1K. When the buffer is full, MS-DOS elimi-
nates the oldest command, making room for the new
command. The buffer contains macros, as well as a
history of commands.

To recall a command in the history, use the following keys:

Key	Function
Up arrow	Displays the preceding command in the history
Down arrow	Displays the next command in the history. When you reach the last command, DOS displays the first command again.
PgUp	Displays the first command in the history
PgDn	Displays the last command in the history

You can use several keys and key combinations to
edit a command on the command line in addition to

the standard DOS editing keys. These keys and key combinations are as follows:

Key(s)	Function
Left arrow	Moves the cursor one character to the left
Ctrl-left arrow	Moves the cursor one word to the left
Right arrow	Moves the cursor one character to the right
Ctrl-right arrow	Moves the cursor one word to the right
Home	Moves the cursor to the first character in the command line
End	Moves the cursor after the last character in the command line
Esc	Erases the current command line
F7	Lists all commands in the history, numbers each command, and indicates the current command
Alt-F7	Erases all the commands in the history
F9	Enables you to specify the number of the command in the history you want to make current. You can press F7 to see the command numbers
F10	Lists all macros in memory
Alt-F10	Erases all macros in memory

DOSKEY enables you to create macros similar to a batch file. By typing the name of a macro, and pressing Enter, you can perform several commands. Note that when you develop macros, you can create a few characters by typing the following dollar sign equivalents:

Code	Description
$g or $G	Redirects output. This code is the same as >.
gg or GG	Appends output. This code is the same as >>.
$l or $L	Redirects input. This code is the same as <.
$b or $B	Pipes the output of one command as the input of a second command. This code is the same as $vb.
$t or $T	Separates macro commands
$$	Uses the dollar sign in the command line
$1 through $9	Specifies replaceable parameters. This code is the same as %1 through %9 in a batch file.
$*	Specifies a replaceable parameter that represents everything typed on the command line after the macro name

When you create a macro, you can include any valid DOS command, including batch files. Although you can start a batch file from a macro, you cannot start a macro from a batch file.

Examples

To start DOSKEY, type DOSKEY.

To create a macro for moving files, type DOSKEY MOVE=COPY $1 $2 $T DEL $1.

To list all macros in memory, type DOSKEY /MACROS.

To use DOSKEY to record batch files, follow these steps:

1. Type the commands you want to record.

2. Type DOSKEY /HISTORY > 123.BAT to save the commands to the batch file.

DOSSHELL

(Start the Shell program) **External**

Starts the Shell that accompanies DOS.

Syntax

To start the DOS Shell in a different screen mode, type *dc:pathc*\DOSSHELL */T:screen /G:screen /B*.

To start the DOS Shell in the default screen mode, type *dc:pathC*\DOSSHELL.

Switches

/T:screen	Displays the DOS Shell in text mode, using the resolution described by the screen
/G:screen	Displays the DOS Shell in graphics mode, using the resolution described by screen
/B	Starts the DOS Shell in black and white rather than color

Switch	Video Display Modes		
	CGA	Monochrome/EGA	VGA
/T:L	25 lines	25 lines	25 lines
/T:M	x	43 lines	43 lines
/T:M1	x	43 lines	43 lines
/T:M2	x	43 lines	50 lines

Switch	Video Display Modes		
	CGA	Monochrome/EGA	VGA
/T:H	x	43 lines	43 lines
/T:H1	x	43 lines	43 lines
/T:H2	x	43 lines	50 lines
/G:L	25 lines	25 lines	25 lines
/G:M	x	43 lines	30 lines
/G:M1	x	43 lines	30 lines
/G:M2	x	43 lines	34 lines
/G:H	x	43 lines	43 lines
/G:H1	x	43 lines	43 lines
/G:H2	x	43 lines	60 lines

Note

The DOS Shell is a user interface that can make DOS easier to use.

EDIT

(Full-screen text editor)   **External**

Enables you to edit text files (such as batch files) in a full-screen mode. This mode gives you much of the editing capability of a simple word processor.

Syntax

> *dc:pathc*\EDIT *d:path**filename.ext* /B /G /H /NOHI

d:path*filename.ext* is the location and the file you want to edit.

Switches

/B	Places EDIT in black-and-white screen colors
/G	Writes quickly to a CGA monitor. This switch may cause "snow" on some monitors.
/H	Displays the maximum lines that your screen supports (43 for EGA and 50 for VGA)
/NOHI	Uses reverse video rather than high-intensity characters (for LCD screens)

Note

EDIT is the text editor that QBasic uses. This program is helpful for creating and editing batch files, as well as other text files. (See also **EDLIN** and **QBASIC**.)

EDLIN

(ASCII text editor)   External

Enables you to edit short batch, text, and data files. MS-DOS 6.0 provides backward compatibility with this limited, line-oriented ASCII text editor. Refer to your DOS manual (prior to DOS version 6) for EDLINs command-line reference. (See also **EDIT**.)

Syntax

*dc:pathc*EDLIN *d:path\filename.ext /b*

d:path\filename.ext is the location and the file you want to edit.

Switch

/b   Instructs EDLIN to ignore any
                            Ctrl-Z character at the end of a
                            file

EMM386

(EMS/UMB provider)   **External**

Emulates expanded memory (EMS 4.0) on an
80386sx, 80386, and 80486 computer. This command
also enables you to place device drivers and TSRs in
reserved memory.

Syntax

To use EMM386 as a device driver, use the following
syntax:

> DEVICE=*dc:pathc*\EMM386.EXE
> *ON|OFF|AUTO memory MIN=size*
> *W=ON|W=OFF Mx|FRAME=xxxx /Pxxxx*
> */Pn=xxxx X=xxxx-xxxx I=xxxx-xxxx B=xxxx*
> *L=minXMS A=altregs H=handles D=xxx*
> *RAM=xxxx-xxxx NOEMS NOVCPI NOHIGHSCAN*
> *VERBOSE WIN=xxxx-xxxx NOHI ROM=xxxx-xxxx*
> *ALTBOOT*

To use EMM386 as a command, use the following
syntax:

> *dc:pathc*\EMM386 *ON | OFF | AUTO W=ON |*
> *W=OFF /?*

ON|OFF|AUTO activates the EMM386 driver (if set
to ON), deactivates the driver (if set to OFF), or
places it in automatic mode (if set to AUTO). The
default is ON.

memory specifies how much extended memory
EMM386 should provide as expanded memory in
addition to the memory used by EMM386 and UMBs.

The default is the amount of free extended memory. Valid values are 64 through 32768K.

MIN=size specifies the minimum amount of extended memory that EMM386 reserves for EMS memory. The default is 256K.

W=ON | W=OFF enables or disables support for the Weitek Coprocessor. The default is W=OFF.

Mx specifies the segment base address. *x* is a number that represents the address. This number is the beginning address of the EMS page frame. The numbers and associated hexadecimal addresses are as follows:

1	C000
2	C400
3	C800
4	CC00
5	D000
6	D400
7	D800
8	DC00
9	E000
10	8000
11	8400
12	8800
13	8C00
14	9000

FRAME=xxxx specifies the beginning address of the EMS page frame. *xxxx* may be one of the addresses listed above.

/Pxxxx specifies the beginning address just as *FRAME=xxxx* does.

Pn=xxxx defines an address for a page segment. Valid values for *n* are 0, 1, 2, 3, 254, and 255. To remain compatible with programs that use EMS 3.2

specifications, P0 through P3 must be contiguous addresses. You cannot use this option if you use *Mx*, *FRAME=xxxx*, or */Pxxxx*.

X=xxxx-xxxx specifies that a range of memory should not be used for the EMS page frame or for UMBs. *xxxx-xxxx* are the memory ranges to keep free. Valid ranges to exclude are in the A000 through FFFF memory ranges.

I=xxxx-xxxx specifies that a range of memory should be used for the EMS page frame or for UMBs. *xxxx-xxxx* are the memory ranges to use. Valid ranges to include are in the A000 through FFFF memory ranges.

B=xxxx specifies the lowest address to use for bank switching. The default is 4000. Valid ranges are 1000 through 4000.

L=xmsmem specifies the number of one-kilobyte sections that remain as extended memory, rather than being converted to EMS memory. *xmsmem* is the value of 1K bytes of memory. In order for 1M to remain as extended memory, use the option L=1024. The default is 0.

A=altregs allocates the number of alternate registers that EMM386 may use. Although the default number is 7, you can specify a number from 0 to 254 for *altregs*.

H=handles enables you to change from the default 64 handles that EMM386 uses. *handles* may be any number from 2 to 255.

D=nnn specifies how much memory to reserve for DMA buffers. The default is 16. You can specify values from 16 through 256.

RAM=xxxx-xxxx specifies memory in the 640K to 1M memory address space to be used for UMBs. If no value is specified, EMM386 uses all extended memory available. Note that the = is required, rather than a hyphen character (-).

NOEMS allocates space in the upper memory area, as in *RAM* and prevents access to expanded memory.

NOVCPI disables support for VCPI applications (applications that use the LIM EMS 3.2 specification). The NOVCPI switch requires that you also use the NOEMS switch; using NOVCPI without NOEMS causes EMM386 to ignore the NOVCPI switch. Using NOVCPI and NOEMS switches overrides the MEMORY and MIN switches.

NOHIGHSCAN limits EMM386's scanning of upper memory for free memory areas in the event you have trouble using EMM386.

VERBOSE allows EMM386 to display status messages and error messages while the driver is loading. The default is OFF.

WIN=xxxx-xxxx reserves a specific memory address range for use by Windows 3.x. Valid areas are in the A000 through FFFF memory ranges.

NOHI prevents EMM386 from loading into the upper memory area, forcing it to load entirely into conventional memory.

ROM=xxxx-xxxx tells EMM386 which ROM areas in upper memory can be shadowed and which areas can speed up systems without shadow RAM. Valid ranges to specify are normally in the A000 through FFFF memory ranges.

ALTBOOT provides an alternate boot sequence for compatibility.

Examples

To install EMM386 from CONFIG.SYS (assuming that EMM386.EXE is in C:\DOS), allocating 1M of EMS memory and enabling reserved memory, type DEVICE=C:\DOS\EMM386.EXE 1024 RAM.

To install EMM386 from CONFIG.SYS (assuming that EMM386.EXE is in C:\DOS), disabling expanded memory, type DEVICE=C:\DOS\EMM386.EXE NOEMS.

To temporarily disable expanded memory, type EMM386 OFF.

To install EMM386 from CONFIG.SYS (assuming that EMM386.EXE is in C:\DOS), disabling expanded memory, including the memory addresses B000-B7FF, and excluding the memory addresses E000 through EFFF, type DEVICE=C:\DOS\EMM386.EXE NOEMS I=B000-B7FF X=E000-EFFF.

Note

You can place device drivers and TSR programs into reserved memory by using the RAM or NOEMS options of EMM386. Use NOEMS only if you do not want to enable expanded memory, but would rather use the extra reserved memory area.

ERASE

(Erase files)   **Internal**

See **DEL**.

EXE2BIN

(Change EXE files into BIN or COM files)   **External**

Changes suitably formatted EXE files into BIN or COM files. MS-DOS 6.0 provides backward compatibility for this command.

Syntax

> *dc:pathc*EXE2BIN *d1:path1/*filename1.*ext1*
>
> *d2:path2/filename2.ext2*

d1: is the name of the disk drive that holds the file you want to convert. *path1/* is the directory of the file you want converted. **filename1** is the root name of the file you want converted. *.ext1* is the extension name of the file you want converted. *d2:* is the name of the disk drive for the output file. *path2/* is the directory of the output file. *filename2* is the root name of the output file. *.ext2* is the extension name of the output file.

Terms

The file you want to convert is the *source* file.

The output file is the *destination* file.

Rules

If you do not specify a drive for the source file, MS-DOS uses the current drive.

If you do not specify a drive for the destination file, MS-DOS uses the source drive.

When you do not specify a path, MS-DOS uses the current directory of the disk.

You must specify a root name for the source file.

If you do not specify a root name for the destination file, MS-DOS uses the root name of the source file.

If you do not specify an extension for the source file, MS-DOS uses the extension .EXE.

If you do not specify an extension for the destination file, MS-DOS uses the extension .BIN.

The EXE file must be in the correct format (following Microsoft conventions).

Note

EXE2BIN is a programming utility that converts EXE (executable) program files to COM or BIN (binary image) files. The resulting program takes less disk space and loads faster.

 EXIT

(Leave secondary command processor)   Internal

Leaves a secondary command processor and returns to the primary command processor.

Syntax

>   EXIT

Note

This command has no effect if a secondary command processor is not loaded or if it was loaded with the /P switch.

EXPAND

(Expand compressed files)   External

Expands compressed program files from the DOS distribution disks. (See also **DECOMP**.)

Syntax

>   EXPAND *d:path*\filename1 *d:path*\filename2

d:path**filename1** is the drive, path, and file name of the file to be expanded. *d:path***filename2** is the drive, path, and file name of the file EXPAND will expand onto your hard disk. You can use wild cards (* and ?).

Rules

If you type EXPAND with no file names specified, DOS asks you for the location and name of the file you want to expand, as well as the location and name you want to give to the expanded file.

If you do not specify a destination directory for a new decompressed file, EXPAND uses the current directory.

FASTHELP

(DOS On-line Help)   External

Provides an on-line summary of help for basic DOS commands and syntax. (See also **HELP**.)

Syntax

FASTHELP *command*

or

command /?

command specifies the particular command you want to see on-line help about. Typing FASTHELP without any command displays an alphabetical list of commands and a brief description of all MS-DOS 6.0 commands.

FASTOPEN

(Fast opening of files)   External

Keeps directory information in memory.

Syntax

To use FASTOPEN as a command, use the following syntax:

*dc:pathc*FASTOPEN d:=nnn ... */X*

In CONFIG.SYS, use the following syntax:

INSTALL=*dc:pathc*FASTOPEN.EXE d:=nnn ... */X*

d: is the name of the disk drive whose directory information should be held in memory. **nnn** is the number of directory entries to be held in memory (10 to 999). **...** designates additional disk drives in the form *d:=nnn*.

Switch

/X	Creates the cache in expanded memory (EMS 4.0 only)

FC

(Compare files)   **External**

Compares two sets of disk files.

Syntax

*dc:pathc*FC */A /C /L /Lb x /N /T /W /xxxx /B*
*d1:path1*filename1.ext1
*d2:path2*filename2.ext2

d1: is the drive that contains the first set of files to be compared. *path1* is the path to the first set of files. **filename1.ext1** is the file name for the first set of files. You can use wild cards.

d2: is the drive containing the second set of files to be compared. *path2* is the path to the second set of files. **filename2.ext2** is the file name for the second set of files. You can use wild cards.

d1 and *d2* and *path1*\ and *path2*\ can be identical. *filename1.ext1* and *filename2.ext2* also can be identical.

Terms

d1:path1\\filename1.ext1 is the *primary file set*.

d2:path2\\filename2.ext2 is the *secondary file set*.

Switches

/A	Abbreviates ASCII comparison displays
/B	Forces a binary file comparison
/C	Causes DOS to disregard the case of letters
/L	Compares files in ASCII mode
/LB x	Sets internal buffer to *x* lines. Also sets maximum number of mismatches before exiting.
/N	Displays line numbers for ASCII comparisons
/T	Suppresses expansion of tabs to spaces
/W	Compresses tabs and spaces
/xxxx	Sets the number of lines (1-9) to match. The default is 2.

Rules

You must specify both the primary and secondary file specifications.

FC checks only normal disk files; it does not check hidden or system files and directories.

Note

Although FC has a function similar to COMP's, FC is a more intelligent file compare utility because it

makes determinations about the files that it compares and assumes that EXE, COM, SYS, OBJ, LIB,
and BIN files are binary. It compares other files as
ASCII files.

FDISK

(Create a hard disk partition)   External

Partitions a hard disk.

Syntax

> *dc:pathc*FDISK */STATUS*

Switch

> /STATUS   Displays a quick view of the
>   partition data of your hard
>   disk

Notes

You must use FORMAT on a newly partitioned drive
after running FDISK.

FDISK/STATUS provides only uncompressed size
partition status for DBLSPACE-compressed drives
and may be incompatible with some third-party
partition schemes.

FIND

(Find string filter)   External

Displays from the designated files all the lines that
match (or do not match) the specified string. This
command also can display the line numbers.

Syntax

> *dc:pathc*\FIND /V/C/N/I "string"
> *d:path*\filename.ext...

"string" is the set of characters for which you want to search. You must enclose the string in quotation marks. **d:** is the name of the disk drive for the file. *path*\ is the directory holding the file. **filename.ext** is the name of the file that you want to search.

Switches

/C	Counts the number of times that **string** occurs in the file, but does not display the lines
/I	Performs a non-case-sensitive search
/N	Displays the line number (number of the line in the file) before each line that contains **string**
/V	Displays all lines that do not contain **string**

FORMAT

(Format disk)   **External**

Initializes a disk to accept MS-DOS information and files. FORMAT also checks the disk for defective tracks and (optionally) places MS-DOS on the disk or hard disk.

Syntax

> *dc:pathc*\FORMAT d: /Q /U /S /1 /8 /B /4
> /F:*size* /N:*sectors* /T:*tracks* /V:*label*

d: is the valid disk drive name.

Switches

/1	Formats only the first side of the floppy disk
/4	Formats a floppy disk in a 1.2M disk drive for double-density (320K/360K) use
/8	Formats an eight-sector floppy disk (V1 compatible)
/B	Formats any disk and leaves enough room on the disk to copy the operating system files to the disk so that the disk can be bootable
/F:size	Formats the disk to less than maximum capacity, with *size* designating one of the following values:

Drive	Allowable Values for Size
160K, 180K	160, 160K, 160KB, 180, 180K, 180KB
320K, 360K	All of above, plus 320, 320K, 320KB, 360, 360K, 360KB
1.2M	All of above, plus 1200, 1200K, 1200KB, 1.2, 1.2M, 1.2MB
720K	720, 720K, 720KB
1.44M	All for 720K, plus 1440, 1440K, 1440KB, 1.44, 1.44M, 1.44MB
2.88M	2880, 2880K, 2880KB, 2.88, 2.88M, 2.88MB

/N:sectors	Formats the disk with the number of sectors you specify, with *sectors* ranging from 1 to 99

/Q	Performs a quick format on the disk, erasing only the file allocation table and root directory. Does not recheck the disk for bad sectors.
/S	Places a copy of the operating system on the disk so that you can boot it
T:tracks	Formats the disk with the number of tracks per side you specify, with tracks ranging from 1 to 999
/V:label	Transfers volume label to formatted disk. Replaces label with 11-character name for new disk.
/U	Formats a disk uncondition-ally. Erases any data that existed on the disk and does not have the ability to recover the information.

Rules

Unless otherwise directed through a switch, MS-DOS formats the disk to its maximum capacity.

Some switches do not work together. For example, you cannot use the following switch combinations:

/V or /S with /B

/V with /8

/N or /T with a 320/360K or hard disk drive

/1, /4, /8, or /B with a hard disk

/Q with /U

FORMAT /U destroys any previously recorded information on the disk.

To use a disk with all versions of MS-DOS, use the /B and /1 switches. (Format the disk for any MS-DOS version and format only one side.)

A volume name can be 1 to 11 characters long and contain any characters that are legal in a file name.

If you use the /S switch (to place the operating system on a disk) and the current directory does not contain a copy of MS-DOS, you are prompted to insert the MS-DOS floppy disk into drive A so that the system receives the copy of the operating system before formatting the disk.

If MS-DOS formats a hard disk that contains a volume label, it asks `Enter current Volume Label for drive d:`. To continue formatting disk drive *d*, enter the disk drive's current volume label. If you do not enter the exact volume label, FORMAT displays `Invalid Volume ID. Format Failure.` FORMAT then aborts the procedure.

If you are formatting a hard disk without a volume label, FORMAT displays `WARNING, ALL DATA ON NON-REMOVABLE DISK DRIVE d: WILL BE LOST! Proceed with Format (Y/N?)`. Answer **Y** to format the hard disk drive, or **N** to abort the format.

Although you can use the /4 switch to create double-sided 5 1/4-inch disks in a high-capacity 5 1/4-inch disk drive, the formatted disk is not reliable when you use it in double-sided disk drives.

GRAFTABL

(Load graphics table)   **External**

Loads into memory the additional character sets to be displayed on the Color Graphics Adapter (CGA). MS-DOS 6.0 provides backward compatibility with this command.

Syntax

To install or change the table used by the CGA, use this command:

*dc:pathc*GRAFTABL codepage

To display the number of the current table, use this command:

*dc:pathc*GRAFTABL /STATUS

codepage is the three-digit number of the code page for the display.

GRAPHICS

(Graphics screen print) **External**

Prints graphics screen contents on suitable printers.

Syntax

*dc:pathc*GRAPHICS type d:path\filename.ext
/R /B /LCD /PRINTBOX:x

type is the type of printer you are using. The printer can be one of the following:

COLOR1	HPDEFAULT	QUIETJETPLUS
COLOR4	LASERJET	RUGGEDWRITER
COLOR8	LASERJETII	RUGGEDWRITERWIDE
DESKJET	PAINTJET	THERMAL
GRAPHICS	QUIETJET	THINKJET
GRAPHICSWIDE		

d:path** is the disk drive and the directory that hold the printer profile file. **filename.ext is the name and location of the printer profile file containing information about the selected printer type.

Switches

/B   Prints the background in color. You can use this switch only when the printer type is COLOR4 or COLOR8.

/LCD	Prints the image as displayed on the PC Convertible's LCD display
/PRINTBOX:x	Prints the image and uses the print box size *id* represented by *x*. This value must match the first entry of a Printbox statement in the printer profile, such as *lcd* or *std*.
/R	Reverses colors so that the image on the paper matches the screen—a white image on black background

Rules

If you use this command to print the graphics screen contents, your printer must be compatible with one of the listed printers.

If you do not specify a **type**, DOS assumes you are using a graphics-capable, dot-matrix printer.

If you do not use the /R (reverse) switch, an inverse image is printed. White images on-screen print as dark colors, and black images print as white.

If you do not use the /B switch, the background color of the screen does not print. The /B switch has no effect unless you specify the printer type COLOR4 or COLOR8.

When you choose the 320-by-200 (medium-resolution) mode, the printer prints in four shades of gray, corresponding to the four possible colors. When you specify the 640-by-200 (high-resolution) mode, the printer prints in black and white, but the printout is rotated 90 degrees to the left. (The upper right corner of the screen is placed on the upper left corner of the printout.)

The only way to deactivate GRAPHICS is to reset your computer.

HELP

(On-line help system)   **External**

Provides on-line, context-sensitive command help.
(See also **FASTHELP**.)

Syntax

   *dc:pathc*HELP */B /G /H /NOHI command*

Switches

/B	Loads the help system in black-and-white mode
command	Specifies a specific command to display help about
/G	Allows CGA screens to update faster
/H	Loads the help system using the maximum number of lines your monitor can display
/NOHI	Disables high intensity display of help text

Note

Typing HELP at the DOS command line displays
the Help Index from which you may highlight any
command listed and press Enter to view the associated help text.

INTERLNK

(Link computers to share resources)   **External**

Allows two computers connected by parallel or
serial ports to share printers, disk drives, and files.

Syntax

To use INTERLNK as a device driver, use the following syntax:

> DEVICE=*dc:pathc*\INTERLNK.EXE */DRIVES:x*
> */NOPRINTER /COMx:address /LPTx:address*
> */AUTO /NOSCAN /LOW /BAUD:xxxx /V*

To use INTERLNK as a command, use the following syntax:

> *dc:pathc*\INTERLNK client:=server:

client: defines the drive letter of the connecting (terminal) drive being redirected to the host (server). **server:** defines the drive letter of the host (server) being redirected.

Switches

/AUTO	Provides INTERLNK with automatic installation if a connection can be established on the server. By default, INTERLNK is installed even if no connection exists (resulting in an error), unless you use this switch.
/BAUD:xxxx	Defines the baud rate for serial communications. Valid values range from 9600 to 115200, with the default at 115200.
/COMx:address	Defines a serial port that you want to redirect, where *x* is the COM port number and *address* is the hexadecimal address of the port (e.g., 3F8 for COM1 and 2F8 for COM2). If you do not specify a port number or address, INTERLNK scans for and uses

the first port it finds on the server. In default mode, INTERLNK scans for all ports unless you specify a particular port.

/DRIVES:x   Defines the number of re-directed drives. The default is 3. If you specify **/DRIVES:0**, INTERLNK only redirects printers.

/LOW   Prevents INTERLNK from loading into upper memory blocks, the default

/LPTx:address   Defines a parallel port that you want to redirect, where *x* is the LPT port number and *address* is the hexadecimal address of the port (e.g., 378 for LPT1 and 278 for LPT2). If you do not specify a port number or address, INTERLNK scans for and uses the first port it finds on the server. In default mode, INTERLNK scans for all ports unless you specify a particular port.

/NOPRINTER   Tells INTERLNK not to redirect printers. By default, INTERLNK redirects all printer ports.

/NOSCAN   Prevents INTERLNK from establishing a connection during setup

/V   Prevents INTERLNK from conflicting with a computer's timer during serial communications or with two computers connected via serial ports

Examples

With both INTERLNK and INTERSVR running, to redirect client drive D: to server drive C, type INTERLNK d=c.

To cancel redirection of drive D, type INTERLNK d=.

Notes

Type INTERLNK at the DOS command line to display the current INTERLNK status.

If you use INTERLNK to connect to a computer system that is not powered up, DOS displays three additional floppy disk drives instead of the contents of the redirected drives. In order to display the contents of drives that have been redirected, use the INTERSVR program (see **INTERSVR**).

INTERLNK reads the LASTDRIVE= setting in your CONFIG.SYS file to determine which drive letter to assign to each redirected drive.

To prevent reassignment of current drive letters, load INTERLNK after all hard drive and RAM drive device drivers.

Using the /NOPRINTER, /LPTx: and /COMx: switches reduces the amount of memory INTERLNK uses as a device driver.

The following DOS commands do not work with INTERLNK: CHKDSK, DEFRAG, DISKCOMP, DISKCOPY, FDISK, FORMAT, MIRROR, SYS, UNDELETE, UNFORMAT.

 INTERSVR

(Start INTERLNK Server)   **External**

Starts the INTERLNK server (see also **INTERLNK**) to allow redirection and status displays.

Syntax

> *dc:path\INTERSVR drive: /X=drive: /*
> *LPT:x | address /COM:xn | address /BAUD:xxxx*
> */B /V /RCOPY*

drive: defines the drive letter of the redirected drive.

Switches

/B	Displays the status screen for the INTERLNK server in black-and-white mode.
BAUD:xxxx	Defines the baud rate for serial communications. Valid values range from 9600 to 115200, with the default at 115200.
/COMx:address	Defines a serial port that you want to redirect, where *x* is the COM port number and *address* is the hexadecimal address of the port (e.g., 3F8 for COM1 and 2F8 for COM2). If you do not specify a port number or address, INTERLNK scans for and uses the first port it finds on the server. In default mode, INTERLNK scans for all ports unless you specify a particular port.
/LPTx:address	Defines a parallel port that you want to redirect, where *x* is the LPT port number and *address* is the hexadecimal address of the port (e.g., 378 for LPT1 and 278 for LPT2). If you do not specify a port number or address, INTERLNK scans for and uses the first port it finds on the server. In default mode, INTERLNK

	scans for all ports unless you specify a particular port.
/RCOPY	Copies files between two computers connected with null modem cables. The MODE command must be on the computer running the INTERLNK program.
/V	Prevents INTERLNK from conflicting with a computer's timer during serial connections.
/X=drive:	Tells INTERSVR to exclude the drive letter specified.

JOIN

(Join disk drives) **External**

Produces a single directory structure by connecting a disk drive to a subdirectory of a second disk drive. MS-DOS 6.0 provides backward compatibility with this command.

Syntax

To connect disk drives, use the following syntax:

dc:pathc\JOIN d1: d2:\directoryname

To disconnect disk drives, use this syntax:

dc:pathc\JOIN d1: /D

To show currently connected drives, use this syntax:

dc:pathc\JOIN

d1: is the name of the disk drive to be connected. **d2:** is the name of the disk drive to which **d1:** is connected. **\directoryname** is the name of a subdirectory in the root directory of d2. **\directoryname** holds the connection to **d1**.

Switch

> /D   Disconnects the specified
> guest disk drive from its host.

Terms

The disk drive being connected is called the *guest disk drive*.

The disk drive and the subdirectory to which the guest disk drive is connected are the *host disk drive* and the *host subdirectory*.

KEYB

(Enable foreign language keys)   **External**

Changes the keyboard layout and characters to one of 18 languages.

Syntax

To change the current keyboard layout, use this syntax:

> *dc:pathc*\KEYB keycode, codepage,
> d:path\KEYBOARD.SYS */E /ID:code*

To display the current values for KEYB, use this syntax:

> *dc:pathc:*\KEYB

keycode is the two-character keyboard code for your location. **codepage** is the three-digit code page that will be used. **d:path** is the drive and the path to the KEYBOARD.SYS file.

Switches

/E	Specifies that you are using an enhanced keyboard. This switch is useful for 8088/8086 computers.
/ID:code	Specifies the enhanced keyboard when the specified country has more than one possible

Example

To change the keyboard layout and characters so that they are appropriate to Latin America, type

KEYB la,437, C:DOS\KEYBOARD.SYS.

Notes

When KEYB is active, it reassigns some alphanumeric characters to different keys and introduces new characters. The new layout and characters vary among the supported languages.

You can find a complete listing of keycodes and codepages in your MS-DOS documentation.

LABEL

(Volume Label)   **External**

Creates, changes, or deletes a volume label for a disk.

Syntax

dc:pathc\LABEL d:volume_label

d: is the name of the disk drive for which you want change the label. **volume_label** is the new volume label for the disk.

LOADFIX

(Fix program load) External

Loads programs just above the first 64K of RAM for compatibility. (See also **SETVER**.)

Syntax

dc:pathc\LOADFIX d:path\filename.ext

d: is the name of the disk drive holding the file to which to apply the command. **path**\ is the path to the file. **filename.ext** is the file name to which to apply the command.

Example

To run the program CAPTURE with LOADFIX, type C:\DOS\LOADFIX C:\UTILS\CAPTURE or LOADFIX CAPTURE.

Note

If the program you are trying to run displays the error message Packed File is Corrupt, try using LOADFIX to correct the problem.

LOADHIGH(LH)

(Load program in reserved memory) Internal

Loads device drivers or memory-resident programs (TSRs) in reserved memory on an 80386sx, 80386, or 80486 computer. (See also **DEVICEHIGH**.)

Syntax

dc:pathc\LOADHIGH d:path\filename.ext
/L:region# prog_options

or

dc:pathc\LH d:path\filename.ext */L:region#*
prog_options

d:path is the location of the device driver or
memory-resident program. **filename.ext** is the name
of the device driver or memory-resident program.
prog_options are any options that **filename.ext**
requires.

Switch

/L:region#   Loads a device driver high
into a specified memory
region

Rules

You must install HIMEM.SYS as a device driver in
CONFIG.SYS.

You must include the statement DOS=UMB or
DOS=HIGH in CONFIG.SYS. (See also **DOS** in the
CONFIG.SYS commands.)

Note

Use this command for those TSR programs you
ordinarily use. You may want to include the
LOADHIGH syntax in your AUTOEXEC.BAT file so
that it is initiated each time you start your system.

MD or MKDIR

(Make directory)   **Internal**

Creates a subdirectory.

Syntax

> MD *d:path*\dirname

or

> MKDIR*d:path*\dirname

d: is the name of the disk drive for the subdirectory. *path* is the valid path name for the path to the directory that will hold the subdirectory. **dirname** is the name of the subdirectory you are creating.

MEM

(Display memory usage)   External

Displays the amount of used and unused memory, allocated and open memory areas, and all programs currently running in memory.

Syntax

> *dc:pathc*\MEM /CLASSIFY /DEBUG /FREE / MODULE name /PAGE

or

> *dc:pathc*\MEM /C /D /F /M name /P

Switches

/CLASSIFY   Displays the programs that are currently loaded in memory, including the memory address, the name, size, and type of each file used for each program, and the amount of conventional and upper program memory that each is using. It also shows the largest free memory block.

/DEBUG	Displays programs and device drivers in memory, including the size in decimal and hexadecimal values, as well as the program or driver name, memory address, size, and type of each file for every program and device driver
/FREE	Displays the free conventional and upper memory areas, the size of each free area, and a summary of all memory use
/MODULE name	Displays information about a specific program currently in memory
/PAGE	Displays any of the above one screen at a time

Note

You can use MEM to display information on how your computer is using memory. MEM displays statistics for conventional memory and also for upper, extended, and expanded memory if available. You cannot specify /CLASSIFY, /DEBUG, /FREE, and /MODULE at the same time.

MEMMAKER

(Optimize memory use)   **External**

Optimizes your computer's memory use by reorganizing device drivers and TSRs in upper memory for optimum fit.

Syntax

> *dc:pathc/*MEMMAKER */B /BATCH /SESSION*
> */SWAP:drive /T /UNDO /W:x,x*

Switches

/B	Runs MEMMAKER in black-and-white mode
/BATCH	Runs MEMMAKER in an unattended (or batch) mode
/SWAP:drive	Tells MEMMAKER what your original startup drive was prior to running MEMMAKER. Use this switch if you use a disk compression program other than Microsoft DoubleSpace or Stacker.
/SESSION	Specifies that MEMMAKER is running in optimize mode (not a user option)
/T	Disables detection of token-ring networks
/UNDO	Tells MEMMAKER to undo the most recently made change to your configuration files
/W:x,x	Specifies upper memory area space for Windows translation buffers if you are running Windows. The default is W:12,12, for two 12K translation buffers. If you are not running Windows, using W:0,0 prevents MEMMAKER from reserving any of the upper memory area.

Examples

To run MEMMAKER in automatic (batch) mode on a black and white display with no Windows translation buffers needed, type MEMMAKER /BATCH /B /W:0,0.

To instruct MEMMAKER to UNDO its last made changes, type MEMMAKER /UNDO.

MIRROR

(Protects against data loss)   **External**

Saves information about a disk drive so that you can recover accidentally lost data. MS-DOS 6.0 provides backward compatibility with this command.

Syntax

To save information about a drive and files that are deleted, use the following syntax:

> dc:pathc\MIRROR d1: d2: dn: /Tdrive-entries /l

To save information about a drive partition, use the following syntax:

> dc:pathc\MIRROR d1: d2: dn: /PARTN

To quit tracking deleted files, use the following syntax:

> dc:pathc\MIRROR /U

d1:, *d2:* and *dn:* are the disk drives for which you want to save information.

Switches

/Tdrive-entries   Loads into memory a portion of MIRROR to keep track of files that you delete. *drive* is the mandatory disk drive for which deleted files are tracked. *entries* is an optional value from 1 to 999 that specifies the maximum number of deleted files that DOS remembers. Default values are as follows:

Disk	Stores
360K	25 entries
720K	50 entries
1.2M or 1.44M	75 entries
20M	101 entries
32M	202 entries
over 32M	303 entries

/l	Keeps MIRROR from making a backup of the mirror file when the file is updated
/PARTN	Makes a copy of the drive's partition table
/U	Removes from memory the memory-resident portion of MIRROR that keeps track of deleted files

Notes

MIRROR creates a hidden file (MIRROR.FIL) on your hard disk that contains a copy of the root directory and file allocation table, which enables you to restore a drive if it is accidentally formatted.

Using the /T switch with MIRROR creates a hidden file called PCTRACKR.DEL and leaves a portion of MIRROR in memory to track deleted files. PCTRACKR.DEL enables you to recover deleted files.

Using the /PARTN switch with MIRROR creates the file PARTNSAV.FIL on a floppy disk. This file contains information from the drive partition table initially created with FDISK. Label the floppy disk and store it in a safe place.

Companion commands for some (not all) of MIRROR functionality are in UNDELETE and UNFORMAT.

MODE

(Set, Devices)   **External**

Sets the mode of operation for the printer(s), the
video display, the keyboard, and the Asynchronous
Communications Adapter. This command also
controls code page switching for the console and
printer.

Syntax

To configure a parallel printer, use this syntax:

> *dc:pathc*\MODE LPT#: cpl, lpi, P

or

> *dc:pathc*\MODE LPT# COLS=cpl LINES=lpi
> RETRY=ret

To set the display mode, use this syntax:

> *dc:pathc*\MODE dt

or

> *dc:pathc*\MODE dt, s, T

or

> *dc:pathc*\MODE CON: COLS=col LINES=line

To configure a serial port, use this syntax:

> *dc:pathc*\MODE COMn: baud, parity, databits,
> stopbits, P

or

> *dc:pathc*\MODE COMn BAUD=baud
> PARITY=parity DATA=databits
> STOP=stopbits RETRY=ret

To redirect the parallel port to the serial port, use
this syntax:

> *dc:pathc*\MODE LPT#: = COMn

To set code pages, use this syntax:

> *dc:pathc*\MODE device CODEPAGE PREPARE
> =((codepage, *codepage*, ...)
> *dp:pathp*\pagefile.*ext*)

or

> *dc:pathc*\MODE device CODEPAGE SELECT
> =codepage

or

> *dc:pathc*\MODE device CODEPAGE REFRESH

or

> *dc:pathc*\MODE device CODEPAGE */STATUS*

To set the keyboards repeat rate, use this syntax:

> *dc:pathc*\MODE CON: RATE=rate
> DELAY=delay

To view the status of a device, use this syntax:

> *dc:pathc*\MODE device /STATUS

#: is the printer number (1, 2, or 3). The colon is optional. **cpl** is the number of characters per line (80 or 132). **lpi** is the number of lines per inch (6 or 8). **P** specifies continuous retries on timeout errors. **ret** specifies one of the following retry actions: E returns an error if the port is busy; P continues retrying; B returns busy if the port is busy; R returns ready if the port is busy; and N is no retry action.

dt is display type, which may be one of the following values: 40, 80, BW40, BW80, CO40, CO80, or MONO. **s** shifts the graphics display right or left one character. **T** requests alignment of the graphics display screen with a one-line test pattern.

col is the number of columns to display on-screen. **lines** is the number of lines to display on-screen. This number is only applicable for an EGA (25 or 43) or VGA (25, 43 or 50) display.

n: is the adapter number (1 or 2). The colon after the number is optional. **baud** is the baud rate (110, 150, 300, 1200, 2400, 4800, or 9600). **parity** is the parity checking (None, Odd, or Even). **databits** is the number of data bits (7 or 8). **stopbits** is the number of stop bits (1 or 2).

device is the name of the device for which code page(s) will be chosen. Valid devices include the following:

CON: The console

PRN: The first parallel printer

LPT#: Any parallel printer (# is 1, 2, or 3)

codepage is the number of the code page(s) to be used with the device. The numbers are as follows:

437   United States

850   Multilingual

860   Portuguese

863   Canadian-French

865   Nordic

... represents additional code pages. *dp:* is the name of the disk drive that contains the code page (font) information. *pathp* is the path to the file containing the code page information. **pagefile**.*ext* is the name of the file containing the code page information. Currently, the provided code page files are as follows:

4201.CPI   IBM Proprinter, Printer XL

4208.CPI   IBM Proprinter X24, Printer XL24

5202.CPI   IBM Quietwriter III printer

EGA.CPI   EGA type displays or IBM PS/2

LCD.CPI   IBM Convertible Liquid Crystal Display

rate is the speed, from 1 to 32, at which characters repeat. The speed varies from 2 cps (characters per second) to 30 cps. **delay** is the number from 1 through 4 that specifies a .25-, .5-, .75-, or 1-second delay before repeating begins.

Switch

/STATUS   Displays the device's setting

MORE

(More output filter)   **External**

Displays one screen of information from the standard input device and pauses and displays the message - -More - -. When you press a key, MORE displays the next screen of information.

Syntax

dc:pathc\MORE

Examples

If you type MORE <TEST.TXT, MORE displays a screenful of information from the file TEST.TXT, and then displays the prompt - -More - - at the bottom of the screen and waits for a keystroke. When you press a key, MORE continues this process until all information has been displayed.

To display the sorted output of the directory command, type DIR I SORT I MORE.

MOVE

(Move files)   **External**

Moves files from one directory or drive to another
directory or drive, optionally renaming the files, and
renames directories.

Syntax

MOVE /Y d1:path1\filename1.*ext1*
d2:path2\filename2.*ext2*

or

MOVE d1:path1\ d2:path2\

or

MOVE d1:*.* d2:

d1: and **d2:** are valid disk drive names. **path1** and
path2** are valid path names. **filename1.*ext1* and
filename2.*ext2* are valid file names.

Terms

The file you are moving (filename1) is called the
source file. The file or directory you are moving the
file to (filename2) is called the *destination directory*
or *destination file*.

Switch

/Y   Moves all files and bypasses
                      user confirmation

Examples

To move the file MYFILE.TXT from the C:\HOLD
directory to the C:\LETTERS directory, type MOVE
C:\HOLD\MYFILE.TXT C:\LETTERS.

To move the file MYFILE.TXT from the C:\HOLD
directory to the C:\LETTERS directory and
rename the file OLDFILE.TXT, type MOVE
C:\HOLD\MYFILE.TXT C:\LETTERS\OLDFILE.TXT.

To move all the files from the C:\HOLD directory to the C:\LETTERS directory, type MOVE
C:\HOLD*.* C:\LETTERS.

To rename the C:\LETTERS directory to C:\DOCS,
type MOVE C:\LETTERS C:\DOCS.

Rules

Any file you move to another directory overwrites a
file with the same name in the new directory.

The MOVE command cannot copy a group of files
into a single new file in a different directory; use
COPY instead.

When renaming directories, you must use the same
directory structure. If you attempt to move a first-
level subdirectory (e.g., C:\DOCS) to a second-level
subdirectory (e.g., C:\DOCS\OLD), the command
fails.

MSAV

(Virus scanning software)　　　　　**External**

Scans for and removes virus-infected files.

Syntax

*dc:pathc\MSAV d:path\ /S /C /R /A /L /N /P /F
/VIDEO /ss /IN /BW /MONO /LCD /FF /BF /NF
/BT /NGM /LE /PS2*

d: path is the drive and directory that you ask
MSAV to scan. If you do not specify a drive or path,
MSAV scans the current drive and path.

Switches

/A	Scans all drives except floppy disk drives A: and B:
/BF	Uses the computer BIOS to display activity on-screen
/BT	Enables you to use a mouse with MSAV in Windows
/BW	Runs MSAV in black-and-white mode
/C	Scans for and removes any viruses found
/F	Prevents display of scanned file names. (You can use this switch with /N and /P.)
/FF	Uses fast screen update mode(CGA)
/IN	Selects a specific color scheme for MSAV
/L	Scans only local (not network) drives
/LCD	Runs MSAV with an LCD color scheme
/LE	Exchanges left and right mouse buttons
/MONO	Runs MSAV in monochrome mode
/N	Runs MSAV in command mode rather than in graphical mode
/NF	Disables use of alternate font sets
/NGM	Runs MSAV without the graphics mouse character
/P	Uses command-line options rather than running MSAV from the graphical interface
/PS2	Resets the mouse if the cursor disappears

/R	Creates a report listing all scanned files and all viruses found and removed and saves the report to the default file MSAV.RPT. By default, this option is off.
/S	Scans selected drives for viruses
/ss	Specifies the number of screen lines your monitor can display, where */ss* is */25*, */28*, */43*, */50*, or */60* depending on the adapter you use
/VIDEO	Shows all the available MSAV display switches

Note

See the MS-DOS 6 Reference Manual for additional information about this program.

MSBACKUP

(Backup and Restore)   **External**

Backs up and restores files from one disk drive or floppy disk to another disk drive or floppy disk. (See also **BACKUP** and **RESTORE**.)

Syntax

> *dc:pathc***MSBACKUP** *setup_name* */BW* */LCD* */MDA*

Switches

/BW	Runs MSBACKUP in black-and-white mode
/LCD	Runs MSBACKUP in LCD mode

| /MDA | Runs MSBACKUP in mono-chrome mode |
| setup_name | Specifies the name of the setup file to use. The default setup file is DEFAULT.SET. |

Rule

You cannot run MSBACKUP from floppy disks.

MSCDEX

(Microsoft CD-ROM Extensions)   **External**

Loads the CD-ROM software extensions in order to access information on CD-ROM discs.

Syntax

*dc:pathc*MSCDEX */D:driver /E /K /S /V /L:letter /M:number*

/D:driver is the drive and driver name of the CD-ROM extension program to load.

Switches

/E	Specifies that MSCDEX use expanded memory for its sector buffers
/K	Specifies that MSCDEX use Kanji support
/L:letter	Specifies the drive letter MSCDEX assigns to the CD-ROM drive
/M:number	Specifies the number of sector buffers MSCDEX uses. The default depends on the drive being buffered.

/S	Loads network server support for the CD-ROM drive
/V	Specifies that MSCDEX displays memory usage statistics when loading

MSD

(Examine technical information)　　　　　**External**

Provides detailed information about your computer hardware, software, and operating environment.

Syntax

*dc:pathc*MSD */I /F d1:path1\\filename /P
d2:path2\\filename /S d3:path3\\filename /B*

d1:, *d2:* , and *d3:* are valid disk drive names. *path1* ,
path2 , and *path3/* are valid path names. *filename1*,
filename2, and *filename3* are valid file names.

Switches

/B	Runs MSD in black-and-white mode
/Fd1:path1\\filename1	Specifies that initial user information be filled out
/I	Prevents MSD from initially trying to determine the hardware it is running on
/Pd2:path1\\filename2	Specifies the drive, directory, and file name where DOS creates the full MSD report
/Sd3:pathc\\filename3	Specifies the drive, directory, and file name where DOS creates the summary MSD report

NLSFUNC

(National language support)   **External**

Provides support for extended country information in MS-DOS and enables you to use the CHCP command. (See also **CHCP**.)

Syntax

*dc:pathc*NLSFUNC **d:path\filename.ext**

d: is the name of the disk drive holding the country information file. **path** is the path to the country information file. **filename.ext** is the name of the file holding the country information. In DOS 6, the file COUNTRY.SYS contains this information.

PATH

(Set directory search order)   **Internal**

Tells MS-DOS to search the specified directories on the specified drives if a program or batch file is not found in the current directory.

Syntax

PATH *d1:path1;d2:path2;d3:path3;...*

d1:, *d2:*, and *d3:* are valid disk drive names. *path1*, *path2*, and *path3* are valid path names to the commands you want to run while in any directory.
... represents additional disk drives and path names.

Note that you are limited to 127 characters.
The default path, if you do not specify one in CONFIG.SYS, is C:\DOS.

POWER

6

(Reduce Power Consumption) **External**

Helps the program conserve power to the system components when devices (monitors, disk drives, etc.) are idle.

Syntax

To use POWER as a device driver, use the following syntax:

DEVICE=*dc:pathc***POWER**

To use POWER as a command, use the following syntax:

dc:pathc**POWER** *[ADV max|reg|min] [STD] [OFF]*

Switches

ADV	Uses Advanced power management specifications. *max* sets POWER to use maximum power conservation; *reg* sets POWER to use regular, or balanced, power conservation (the default); *min* sets POWER to use minimum power conservation.
STD	Specifies that POWER use the computer's built-in Advanced Power Management hardware to conserve power

Note

If the computer using POWER does not support the Advanced Power Management specification, setting POWER to *STD* disables power management functions.

PRINT

(Background printing)   **External**

Prints a list of files while the computer performs other tasks.

Syntax

> *dc:pathc*PRINT */D:device /B:bufsiz /U:busytick*
> */M:maxtick /S:timeslice /Q:maxfiles*
> *d1:path1\\filename1.ext1 /T /C /P*
> *d2:path2\\filename2.ext2 /T /C /P ...*

d1: and *d2:* are valid disk drive names. *path1* and *path2* are valid path names to the files for printing. *filename1.ext1* and *filename2.ext2* are the names of the files you want to print. You can use wild cards. ... represents additional valid file names in the form of *dx:pathx\\filenamex.extx*.

Switches

You can use the following switches when you first issue PRINT:

/B:bufsize	Specifies the size of the buffer in bytes
/D:device	Specifies the device to use
/M:maxtick	Sets the maximum number of clock ticks to use
/Q:maxfiles	Sets the maximum number of files to queue
/S:timeslice	Sets the number of times per second that PRINT can print (number of timeslices)
/U:busytick	Specifies the number of clock ticks to wait for the printer

You can use the following switches any time you issue PRINT:

/C	Cancels the printing of the file
/P	Adds files to the print queue
/T	Terminates printing of all files

PROMPT

(Set the System Prompt)   Internal

Customizes the MS-DOS prompt.

Syntax

> PROMPT promptstring

promptstring is the text for the new system prompt.

Rules

Any text entered for **promptstring** becomes the new system prompt.

You may enter special characters with the metastrings.

The new system prompt stays in effect until you restart MS-DOS or reissue the PROMPT command.

Metastrings

A metastring is a group of characters transformed into another character or characters. To use certain characters (for example, the < or > I/O redirection symbols), you must enter the appropriate meta-string to place the desired character(s) in your promptstring. Otherwise, MS-DOS immediately attempts to interpret the character.

All metastrings begin with the dollar sign ($) and consist of two characters, including the $. The following list contains metastring characters and their meanings:

Character	Produces
$	$, the dollar sign
_ (underscore)	A new line (moves to the first position of the next line)
b	|, the vertical bar
d	The date, same as the DATE command
e	The escape character
g	>, the greater-than character
h	The backspace character which erases the previous character
l	<, the less-than character
n	The current disk drive
p	The current disk drive and path, including the current directory
q	=, the equal sign
t	The time, same as the TIME command
v	The version number of MS-DOS

If you type any other character, DOS ignores it.

Examples

To change the prompt to display the current drive, path, and a greater-than sign (C:\DOS>), type
PROMPT pg.

To change the prompt to display the date on one line and the drive and path in brackets on the second line, type **PROMPT d_[$p]**.

To reset the prompt to the default (C>), type **PROMPT**.

Note

To see the text of PROMPT after it has been set, use the SET command. The default prompt in a clean boot (F5) and an interactive boot(F8) is pg.

QBASIC

(Basic Interpreter)   **External**

Loads the BASIC interpreter into memory for BASIC programming.

Syntax

> *dc:pathc***QBASIC** *d:path\\filename.ext /H /NOHI /B /EDITOR /G /MBF /RUN*

d:path is the optional location of the BASIC program to load into memory. *filename.ext* is the name of the BASIC program.

Switches

/B	Places QBASIC in black-and-white mode
/EDITOR	Starts the editor in nonprogramming mode
/G	Enables a CGA monitor to update quickly. Do not use this switch if "snow" appears on-screen.

/H	Changes the display mode to view QBASIC with the maximum number of lines on-screen
/MBF	Enables the QBASIC statements CVS, CVD, MKS\$, and MKD\$ to use the Microsoft Binary Format for numbers
/NOHI	Enables QBASIC to work with monitors that do not support high-intensity video
/RUN	Loads and runs the program

RD or RMDIR

(Remove directory)   **Internal**

Removes a subdirectory.

Syntax

> **RMDIR d:path**

or

> **RD d:path**

d: is the name of the drive holding the subdirectory.
path is the name of the path to the subdirectory.
The last path name is the subdirectory you want to
delete.

Note

The directory must be empty before you can
remove it.

RECOVER

(Recover files or disk directory)   External

Recovers a file that contains bad sectors or a file
from a disk with a damaged directory. MS-DOS 6.0
provides backward compatibility with this command. (See also **UNDELETE**.)

Syntax

To recover a file, use the following syntax:

> *dc:pathc*\RECOVER d:path\filename.ext

To recover a disk with a damaged directory, use the
following syntax:

> *dc:pathc*\RECOVER d:

d: is the name of the disk drive holding the damaged
file or floppy disk. **path** is the path to the directory
holding the file to be recovered. **filename.ext** is the
file to be recovered. You can use wild cards, but
DOS recovers only the first file that matches the
wild card file name.

REN or RENAME

(Rename file)   Internal

Changes the name of the disk file(s).

Syntax

> RENAME *d:path*\filename1.*ext1* filename2.*ext2*

or

> REN *d:path*\filename1.*ext1* filename2.*ext2*

d: is the name of the disk drive holding the file(s) to be renamed. *path* is the path to the file(s) to be renamed. **filename1**.*ext1* is the current name of the file. You can use wild cards. **filename2**.*ext2* is the new name for the file. You can use wild cards.

REPLACE

(Replace/update files)   **External**

Selectively replaces files with matching names from one disk to another. Selectively adds files from one disk to another.

Syntax

> *dc:pathc*REPLACE *ds:paths*filenames.*exts*
> **dd:pathd** */A/P/R/S/W/U*

ds: paths/ is the name of the drive and directory holding the files to be replaced. **filenames**.*exts* is the name of the files to be replaced. You can use wild cards.

dd: is the name of the disk drive holding the replacement files. **pathd** is the path to the replacement files.

Terms

The file that adds to or that replaces another file is the *source*, represented by an *s* in the name (*ds:paths***filenames**.*exts*).

The file that is replaced or the disk and directory that contains the added file is the *destination*, represented by the letter d (**dd:pathd**). MS-DOS refers to this as the *target*.

Switches

/A	Adds files from source that do not exist on the destination
/P	Prompts and asks whether the file should replace or add to the destination
/R	Replaces read-only files
/S	Replaces files in the current directory and subdirectories beneath this directory
/W	Waits for you to insert the source floppy disk
/U	Replaces only those files of a date and time earlier than the source files

RESTORE

(Restore backed up files)   External

Restores one or more backup files from a floppy disk or hard disk onto another floppy disk or hard disk. This command complements the BACKUP command. This command has backward compatibility with MS-DOS 6.0. (See also **MSBACKUP**.)

Syntax

RESTORE d1:*path1\filename1.ext1*
d2:*path2\filename2.ext /S /P /M /N /B:date
/A:date /L:time /E:time /D*

d1: is the name of the disk drive holding the backup file(s). **d2:** is the disk drive to receive the restored file(s). *path\ filename.ext* is the path and file name of source files to restore and the path and file name of the destination of the restored files. You can use wild cards. A RESTORE path name can exist on the disks holding the backed up files.

Switches

/A:date	Restores all files created or modified on or after the date you enter. Enter the date in the same format as the date in the /B switch (MMDDYY).
/B:date	Restores all files created or modified on or before the date you enter
/D	Displays files that match the file specification without restoring files
/E:time	Restores all files modified at or earlier than the specified time
/L:time	Restores all files modified at or later than the specified time. The time format is *hh:mm:ss*, where *hh* is the hour, *mm* is the minutes, and *ss* is the seconds.
/M	Restores all files modified or deleted since the backup set was made. This switch is like the /N switch because /M processes files that no longer exist on the destination, but /M also restores files that have been modified since the last backup.
/N	Restores all files that no longer exist on the destination. This switch is like the /M switch, but /N processes only the files deleted from the destination since the backup set was made.

/P	Asks whether a file should be restored if it is marked as read-only or has been changed since the last backup
/S	Restores files in the directory specified and all other sub-directories below it. This switch is identical to BACKUP's /S switch.

 SET

(Set/show environment) **Internal**

Sets or shows the system environment.

Syntax

To display the environment, use the following syntax:

    SET

To add to or alter the environment, use the following syntax;

    SET name=string

name is the name of the string you want to add to the environment. **string** is the information you want to store in the environment.

Term

The *environment* is an area in RAM memory reserved for alphanumeric information that MS-DOS commands or user programs may examine and use.

Note

You can use SET to set environment strings in CONFIG.SYS with version 6.

SETVER

(Emulate previous DOS versions)   **External**

Enables the current DOS version to emulate an older DOS version so that the current version can run a certain program file. (See **SETVER** in CONFIG.SYS Commands.)

Syntax

To add a program to the version table, use the following syntax:

dc:pathc\SETVER *d:* filename.ext dosver

To remove a program from the version table, use the following syntax:

dc:pathc\SETVER filename.ext /DELETE

To view the version table, use the following syntax:

dc:pathc\SETVER

d: is the drive that contains the DOS system files. **filename.ext** is the program file to add to the version table. **dosver** is a valid version of DOS previous to DOS 6 (5.00, 4.01, 4.00, 3.30, 3.20, and so on).

Switches

/DELETE	Removes a program and its associated DOS version from the version table. You can abbreviate this switch as /d.
/QUIET	Displays no messages. Works with /DELETE only.

Note

SETVER enables programs requiring specific DOS versions to operate with DOS V6. When you use

SETVER, the current version table is affected. The change is not active until you restart DOS, however. Specifying a file that is already in the version table modifies the file's settings.

SHARE

(Check shared files)   **External**

Enables MS-DOS support for file and record locking.

Syntax

*dc:pathc*SHARE */F:name_space /L:numlocks*

Switches

/F:name_space	Sets the amount of memory space (name_space) used for file sharing
/L:numlocks	Sets the maximum number (numlocks) of file/record locks SHARE can use at one time

Rules

If you do not specify the */F* switch, *name_space* is set to 2,048 bytes. Each open file uses 11 bytes plus its full file specification (disk drive name, path name, and file name). The 2,048 bytes can contain 27 files that use all 63 characters available for the full file name.

If you do not specify the */L* switch, SHARE uses the default of 20 simultaneous file locks.

Load SHARE only once after MS-DOS starts. If you attempt to load SHARE again, MS-DOS displays an error message.

SHARE normally increases the size of MS-DOS by approximately 4,900 bytes. If the number of locks (/L switch) or amount of memory space (/F switch) increases or decreases, the size of MS-DOS also increases or decreases proportionately.

The only way to remove SHARE is to restart MS-DOS.

If you have not given the FCBS command in your CONFIG.SYS file, SHARE adjusts the file control block (FCB) table as if you gave the command FCBS = 16,8.

Note

You use SHARE when two or more programs or processes share the files of a single computer, whether through a network or a multitasking program such as Windows 3.1. After SHARE loads, MS-DOS checks each file for locks whenever it is opened, read, or written. If a file has been opened for exclusive use, a second attempt to open the file produces an error. If one program locks a portion of a file, another program attempting to read, write, or read and write the locked portion creates an error.

SORT

(Sort string filter)   **External**

Reads lines from the standard input device, performs an ASCII sort of the lines, and then writes the lines to the standard output device. The sorting may be in ascending or descending order and may start at any column in the line.

Syntax

   dc:pathc\SORT /R /+c

Switches

/R	Sorts in reverse order. The letter Z comes first, and the letter A comes last.
/+c	Starts sorting with column number c

Examples

To sort the lines in the file WORDS.TXT and display the sorted lines on-screen, type SORT < WORDS.TXT.

To sort the lines in the file WORDS.TXT in reverse order and display the lines on-screen, type SORT < WORDS.TXT /R.

To start sorting at the eighth character in each line of WORDS.TXT and display the output on-screen, type SORT /+8 < WORDS.TXT.

To display the directory information sorted by file size (the file size starts in the 14th column), type DIR | SORT /+14. Unfortunately, other lines, such as the volume label, are also sorted starting at the 14th column.

SUBST

(Substitute path name)   External

Creates an alias disk drive name for a subdirectory. This command is used principally with programs that do not use path names.

Syntax

To establish an alias, use the following syntax:

dc:pathc\SUBST d1: d2:pathname

To delete an alias, use the following syntax:

dc:pathc\SUBST d1: /D

To see the current aliases, use the following syntax:

dc:pathc\SUBST

d1: is a valid disk drive name that becomes
the alias. **d1:** may be a nonexistent disk drive.
d2:pathname is a valid disk drive name and directory path that will be nicknamed **d1:**.

Switch

/D   Deletes the alias

Examples

To have DOS actually use the directory C:\BIN when
you use disk drive name E, type SUBST E: C:\BIN.

If the current directory of drive C is \WORDS, you
can substitute Drive F for the directory C:\WORDS
\LETTERS by typing SUBST F: C:LETTERS. Because
\WORDS is the current directory, MS-DOS finds
LETTERS as the subdirectory of WORDS. MS-DOS
adds \WORDS\ to the alias.

To delete the alias F:, type SUBST F: /D. Afterward,
the use of F: produces an error message from
MS-DOS.

SYS

(Place operating system on disk)   **External**

Places a copy of MS-DOS on the specified floppy disk
or hard disk.

Syntax

dc:pathc\SYS d1: d2:

d1: is the disk drive to receive the copy of MS-DOS.
d2: is the disk drive that contains the copy of
MS-DOS.

Rule

The destination disk cannot contain data or have
been formatted with the */S* or */B* option of the
FORMAT command.

Note

The SYS command places a copy of IO.SYS and
MSDOS.SYS on the targeted disk. To make the disk
bootable (able to load and execute the disk operating system), you must also copy COMMAND.COM.

TIME

(Set/show the time)   **Internal**

Sets and shows the system time.

Syntax

To set the time, use the following syntax:

TIME hh:mm:ss.xx

To show the time, use the following syntax:

TIME

hh is a one- or two-digit number for hours (0 to 23).
mm is a one- or two-digit number for minutes (0 to
60). **ss** is a one- or two-digit number for seconds
(0 to 60). **xx** is a one- or two-digit number for
hundredths of a second (0 to 99). You can specify
only hours and minutes.

Note

Depending on the setting of the country code in your CONFIG.SYS file, a comma may be the separator between seconds and hundredths of seconds.

TREE

(Display all directories)   External

Displays all the subdirectories on a disk and optionally displays all the files in each directory.

Syntax

> *dc:pathc*\TREE d: /F /A

d: is the disk drive holding the disk you want to examine.

Switches

/A	Uses ASCII characters rather than linedraw characters to display the connection of subdirectories
/F	Displays all files in the directories

TYPE

(Type file on-screen)   Internal

Displays the contents of the file on-screen.

Syntax

> TYPE *d:path*\filename.*ext*

d: is the name of the disk drive holding the file to display. *path*\ is the MS-DOS path to the file.

filename.*ext* is the name of the file to display.
You cannot use wild cards.

UNDELETE

(Restore deleted files/directories)   **External**

Restores deleted files and directories.

Syntax

>   *dc:pathc*UNDELETE **d:path\filename.ext** */DT*
>   */DS /DOS*

or

>   *dc:pathc*UNDELETE */LIST /ALL /PURGE:drive*
>   */STATUS /LOAD /UNLOAD /DOS /DT /OS*
>   */Sentry:drive /Tracker:drive-entries*

d:path is the drive and subdirectory location of the
file you want to restore. **filename.ext** is the name of
the file you want to restore.

Switches

/ALL	Recovers all files without prompting. UNDELETE uses the delete tracking file, if one exists. Otherwise UNDELETE uses the standard DOS directory. If UNDELETE uses the DOS directory, # replaces the missing first character. If a second file name conflicts with an already restored file, then another character replaces the #.

/DOS	Specifies UNDELETE to restore files based on the directory contents. You must confirm each file before UNDELETE restores it. If a delete tracking file exists, UNDELETE ignores it.
/DS	Restores files based on the information in the delete sentry directory
/DT	Restores files based on the information in the delete tracking file
/LIST	Displays the files that may be recovered. If you specify a file or files to be recovered, the list is limited by the file name.
/LOAD	Loads into memory the resident portion of UNDELETE as defined in the UNDELETE.INI file
/PURGE:drive	Deletes all the files in the SENTRY directory
/Sentry:drive	Loads into memory a portion of UNDELETE to keep track of files that you delete. *drive* is the mandatory disk drive for which deleted files are tracked. You can specify multiple drives.
/STATUS	Shows what level of UNDELETE protection is currently enabled

/Tracker:drive-entries	Loads into memory a portion of UNDELETE to keep track of files that you delete. *drive* is the mandatory disk drive for which deleted files are tracked. *entries* is an optional value from 1 to 999 that specifies the maximum number of files that are remembered when deleted. Default values are as follows:

Disk	Stores
360K	25 entries
720K	50 entries
1.2M	75 entries
1.44M	75 entries
20M	101 entries
32M	202 entries
over 32M	303 entries

/UNLOAD	Removes from memory the memory-resident portion of UNDELETE that keeps track of deleted files

Note

When you delete a file, DOS removes the first character in the file name. If you undelete using the \DOS switch, DOS prompts you to specify the actual character that should replace the missing first character. If you use the /ALL switch, and a delete tracking file does not exist, each deleted file is restored without prompting.

UNFORMAT

(Recover a formatted disk)   **External**

Reconstructs a formatted floppy disk.

Syntax

>   *dc:pathc***UNFORMAT** **d:** */L /TEST /P*

d: is the drive on which UNFORMAT acts.

Switches

/L	Lists on-screen all files and subdirectories that UNFORMAT finds
/P	Prints a list of all files and subdirectories that UNFORMAT finds
/TEST	Performs a simulated unformat of the disk

Notes

UNFORMAT attempts to recover a formatted disk using the files created by UNDELETE or the file created by a safe format.

To use UNFORMAT, you should format a floppy disk using FORMAT /S, and transfer the UNFORMAT.EXE, AUTOEXEC.BAT, and CONFIG.SYS to the floppy disk. Also, transfer to the floppy disk any device drivers that are necessary for the computer's operation. You may need to edit AUTOEXEC.BAT and CONFIG.SYS to read files from the floppy disk.

Before using UNFORMAT, use UNFORMAT with the /TEST switch. This procedure helps you to determine whether your UNDELETE files are up-to-date, or if UNFORMAT will perform to your expectations.

VER

(Display version number)   Internal

Shows the MS-DOS version number on the video display.

Syntax

VER

VERIFY

(Set/show disk verification)   Internal

Sets the computer to check the accuracy of data written to the disk(s) to ensure that information is properly recorded, and shows whether the data has been checked.

Syntax

To show the verify status, use the following syntax:

VERIFY

To set the verify status, use the following syntax

VERIFY ON

or

VERIFY OFF

Rules

VERIFY accepts only one of two parameters: ON or OFF.

When VERIFY is ON, it remains on until one of the following occurs:

- You issue a VERIFY OFF.

- A SET VERIFY system call turns off the command.

- You restart MS-DOS.

Note

VERIFY does not affect any other MS-DOS operation. Although VERIFY assures the integrity of the recorded data, verifying the data also takes extra time.

(Display volume label)   **Internal**

Displays the volume label of the disk, if the label exists.

Syntax

VOL *d:*

d: is the name of the disk drive whose label you want to display.

(Virus protection)   **External**

Provides continuous virus protection, monitoring, and detection.

Syntax

dc:pathc\VSAFE */OPTION* #+- */NE /NX /An /Cn /N /D /U*

Switches

/An	Sets the hot key to ALT and another key. *n* specifies the new hot key to press with ALT.
/Cn	Sets the hot key to Ctrl and another key. *n* specifies the new hot key to press with ALT.
/D	Disables VSAFE's check - summing (CRC) procedure
/N	Allows VSAFE to monitor network drives
/NE	Prevents VSAFE from loading into expanded memory
/NX	Prevents VSAFE from loading into extended memory
/OPTION#+-	Specifies which options to enable or disable for VSAFE operation. + enables an option and - disables an option. Valid options are as follows:

Number	Function
1	Warns you when you issue a formatting request
2	Warns you when a program attempts to remain memory-resident
3	Disables writes to disk.

Number	Function
4	Checks all files that MS-DOS opens
5	Checks all disks and drives for virus infection in the boot sector
6	Warns you when a program attempts to access and write to the boot sector or partition table of a hard disk drive
7	Warns you when a program attempts to access and write to the boot sector of a floppy disk
8	Warns you when a program attempts to change an executable file

/U	Unloads VSAFE from memory

(Extended COPY)   **External**

Selectively copies files from one or more subdirectories.

Syntax

> *dc:pathc*XCOPY *ds:paths\filenames.exts*
> *dd:pathd\filenamed.extd /A /D:date /E /M /P /S*
> */V /W*

ds: is the name of the disk drive holding the files
to be copied. *paths* is the path to the files to be
copied. *filenames.exts* is the name of the file(s) to
be copied. You can use wild cards.

dd: is the name of the disk drive that will receive
the copied files. (MS-DOS refers to it as the target.)
pathd is the path that will receive the copied files.
filenamed.extd is the name to be given to the copied
files. You can use wild cards.

Switches

/A	Copies files with archive flags set to on (the file has been created or modified since the last running of BACKUP or XCOPY). /A does not reset the file's archive flag.
/D:date	Copies files created or modified since the *date* you enter. This option is identical to BACKUP's /D switch.
/E	When given with the /S switch, causes XCOPY to create empty subdirectories on the destination if the subdirectory on the source is empty. If you do not give the /E switch, /S ignores empty directories.
/M	Copies files with archive flags set to on (the file has been created or modified since the last running of BACKUP or XCOPY). /M resets the file's archive flag.

/P	Pauses and asks for confirmation before copying each file
/S	Copies the files in the source directory and all files in subsequent subdirectories. This option is identical to BACKUP's and RESTORE's /S switch.
/V	Verifies that the files have been copied correctly (identical to COPY's /V switch)
/W	Waits until you change the floppy disk. XCOPY prompts you to change floppy disks before it searches for the files to copy.

BATCH FILES

A batch file provides a shortcut for executing one or many MS-DOS commands. When you type just the name of a batch file, the file executes each line as if you had entered the line from the keyboard.

Batch files can automate long or repetitive instructions. These files reduce the chance you might mistype a command, and you can start lengthy tasks and leave them to run unattended.

You can view writing batch files as a way of programming in MS-DOS. This section indicates the procedure for creating batch files, explains the batch subcommands, and gives examples of batch files you can use.

Creating Batch Files

You can create batch files by using COPY CON, any word processor capable of creating text files (most can), or a text editor (including the MS-DOS EDIT editor). You should not use COPY CON for the longer examples, however, because correcting typographical errors is not easy in these situations.

If you use a word processor, use the programmer or nondocument mode, or save the file as an ASCII file. The normal mode of many word processors stores the characters you type in a code that MS-DOS may not understand. If your word processing program does not distinguish between documents and nondocuments, use the following method to create a test batch file:

1. Type a simple batch file like those that this section explains. Each line of the file must be a single, executable MS-DOS command. Avoid underlining, bold, and other special formatting. Make sure that no hard return or other symbols appear on-screen.

2. Save the batch file with a file extension of BAT; then try to run it at the MS-DOS prompt.

    If a Bad command or file name message appears, consult your word processor's manual. Look up ASCII files to see how the program stores files in ASCII or nondocument mode. If no information is available, contact the software publisher to find out how to write batch files with the program.

The batch files given in this section are typed in all capital letters. MS-DOS accepts lowercase letters except in special cases that are pointed out in the text.

Rules for Creating Batch Files

The batch file's root name can range from one to eight characters in length and must conform to the DOS rules for creating file names. You must use the file name extension .BAT.

A batch file should not have the same root name as that of a program file (a file ending with .COM and .EXE) in the current directory. Nor should you use an internal MS-DOS command, such as COPY or DATE, as a root name. If you use one of these root names to name a batch file, and then try to run the batch file, MS-DOS executes the program or the command instead.

You can enter any valid MS-DOS system-level commands. You also can use the parameter markers (%0-%9) or environmental variables by enclosing the variable name in percent signs (such as %COMSPEC%).

You can enter any valid batch subcommand.

To use the percent sign (%) for a file name in a command, enter the percent symbol twice. For example, to use a file called A100%.TXT, you enter A100%%.TXT. This rule does not apply to the parameter markers (0%-9%) or environmental variables.

You can suppress the display of any line from the batch file if an @ or a ; is the first nonspace character on the line.

Executing Batch Files

You execute a batch file by entering the batch-file name at the MS-DOS prompt, using the following syntax:

*dc:pathc*filename *parameters*

dc: is the name of the disk drive that holds the batch file. *pathc* is the path to the batch file. **filename** is the batch file's root name. *parameters* are the parameters the batch file uses.

Rules for Executing Batch Files

To invoke a batch file, type its root name. For example, to invoke the batch file OFTEN.BAT, type **OFTEN**, and then press **Enter**.

MS-DOS executes each command one line at a time. DOS substitutes the specified parameters for the markers when it uses the command.

MS-DOS recognizes a maximum of 10 parameters. If you do not want to be limited to this number of parameters, use the SHIFT subcommand.

If MS-DOS encounters an incorrectly phrased batch subcommand, DOS displays a Syntax error message, and then continues executing the remaining commands in the batch file.

To stop a running batch file, press **Ctrl-Break** or **Crtl-C**. MS-DOS displays this message: Terminate batch job (Y/N)?_. If you press **Y**, DOS ignores the rest of the commands, and the system prompt appears. If you press **N**, MS-DOS skips the current command but processes the other commands in the file.

MS-DOS remembers which directory holds the batch file. Your batch file may cause the current directory to change at any time.

MS-DOS remembers which floppy disk holds the batch file, and you can change floppy disks at any time. MS-DOS prompts you to insert the floppy disk that holds the batch file, if necessary.

You can make MS-DOS execute a second batch file immediately after the first one is finished. Enter the name of the second batch file as the last command in the first batch file. You also can execute a second batch file within the first batch file and return to the first batch file by using the CALL subcommand.

Batch subcommands are valid only for batch files. With the exception of FOR..IN..DO, you cannot execute batch file subcommands as normal MS-DOS commands.

Although you cannot redirect the input or output of a batch file, you can use redirection in the lines within a batch file.

When MS-DOS executes the AUTOEXEC.BAT file after the computer boots, the system does not automatically request the date and time. To get the current date and time, you must put the DATE and TIME commands in the AUTOEXEC.BAT file.

Starting a Program with a Batch File

You probably use the same programs each day. To start each program, you must type several DOS commands. To speed up this process, you can create a batch file. Suppose that you want to create a batch file that starts Lotus 1-2-3. Create the following batch file and place it on your search path:

    CD\123

    123

    XCOPY C:\DATA\123 A:/M

    CD\

Select a name appropriate to the batch file action. In this case, name the file 123.BAT. To start the batch file, type 123 and press Enter.

Creating a Batch File Using DOSKEY

DOSKEY is a terminate-and-stay-resident program that manages the commands you type at the command line. The number of commands DOSKEY remembers depends on the amount of memory you allocate to DOSKEY.

After you type several commands at the command line, you can reuse each command by pressing the up arrow key to recall a past command. When you use the /HISTORY switch with DOSKEY, all the commands that DOSKEY can remember are listed on-screen. Using redirection, you can save the commands to a file.

Suppose that each day you use the BACKUP command to copy files from the C:\LTR directory to backup disks after you erase all backup files created by your word processor. From the command line, start DOSKEY by typing DOSKEY and pressing Enter.

Next, type the commands you use on a daily basis. For example, type the following:

    DEL C:\LTR*.BAK

    BACKUP C:\LTR A:

To save these commands to a batch file called BACKLTR.BAT, type DOSKEY /HISTORY > BACKLTR.BAT. The history of the two commands is redirected to become the contents of a file, BACKLTR.BAT.

Using CLS to Clear the Screen

Running several DOS utilities in a row may leave information on-screen and may make it difficult for you to find the information you need. The CLS command removes unwanted information from the screen. The CLS command often is included in a batch file as follows:

    ECHO OFF

    CLS

The screen clears and ECHO OFF suppresses the display of commands.

Defining Parameters

The information you type after the command is called a *parameter*. Within a batch file, you can define up to 10 parameters. You define a parameter within the batch file by using a *variable marker*. A variable is a percent sign (%) followed by a number from 0 to 9. Variables are called markers, replaceable parameters, or arguments.

Examples

Consider the file MOVE.BAT. This batch file copies a file to a designated subdirectory and then erases the original file:

```
@ECHO OFF
COPY %1 %2 /V
DEL C:\%1
```

Suppose that you type the following command line:

```
MOVE C:\DATA\123\SCHEDULE.WK1
C:\DATA\HOURS
```

The batch file MOVE.BAT begins executing and DOS replaces each parameter marker with the respective parameter. The batch file executes as follows:

```
@ECHO OFF
COPY C:\DATA\123\SCHEDULE.WK1
C:\DATA\HOURS/V
DEL C:\DATA\123\SCHEDULE.WK1
```

DOS copies SCHEDULE.WK1 from C:\DATA\123 to C:\DATA\HOURS and verifies the file as it copies. You can modify MOVE.BAT with the SHIFT command so that you can specify on one line the movement of several files. The new MOVE.BAT file follows:

```
@ECHO OFF
:LOOP
IF "%2" =.="" GOTO END
ECHO Moving %1 to %2
COPY %1 %2 /V
DEL %1
SHIFT
SHIFT
GOTO LOOP
:END
```

The syntax for using this batch file is as follows:

> **MOVE source1 destination1source2
> destination2...**

Notice that you can type pairs of source and destination files. The batch file uses IF to make sure that you entered parameters. If the second parameter (%2) is empty, the batch file goes to END (the batch file quits). If the second parameter is not empty, DOS copies the source file to the destination and then deletes the source file.

The two SHIFT commands throw away the first pair of source and destination parameters. The second pair of parameters become %1 and %2, respectively. The batch file returns to the label :LOOP, and the entire process starts again.

Counting Parameters

A batch file has 10 possible parameters: %0 through %9. The first parameter,%0, signifies the name of the batch file you type at the MS-DOS prompt. When you use replaceable parameters, remember to start with %1, not with %0.

The remaining items on the line are parameters 1 through 9. The first word after the batch file name is parameter number 1, %1 in the file. The second word is %2, and the ninth item on the line is %9. Each word on the line is separated from the next by a space, comma, colon, semicolon, single quotation mark, or equal sign.

Although MS-DOS restricts you to parameters 0 to 9 within a batch file, a command line can have many parameters within its 127-character limit. See the explanation of the SHIFT subcommand to learn how to trick MS-DOS into using the other arguments.

Batch File Commands

You can use any valid MS-DOS command in a batch file. MS-DOS also has a set of commands specifically for use in batch files: the batch subcommands. The batch subcommands follow.

CALL

Runs a second batch file, and then returns control to the first batch file.

Syntax

CALL *dc:pathc*filename parameters

Notes

Use the CALL command to run a second batch file from another batch file. When the second batch file is finished, MS-DOS continues processing the remaining commands in the first batch file.

If you do not use CALL to run the second batch file, MS-DOS concludes batch-file processing when the second file finishes. MS-DOS does not usually return to the first batch file.

CHOICE

Displays specific messages and pauses for user response. Errorlevel responses are returned to the batch file for processing.

Syntax

CHOICE */C:keystroke /N /S /T:a,ss text*

Switches

/C:keystroke	Specifies which characters are acceptable as responses to CHOICE parameters. The default, without using /C, is Y or N for a Yes/No prompt.
/N	Prevents DOS from displaying prompts while leaving the acceptable keystrokes valid
/S	Allows case sensitivity in keystrokes
/T:a,ss	Allows a pause after a CHOICE issues a parameter. *a* specifies the default alphabetical character that DOS chooses if the user does not press a key. *ss* specifies the number of seconds that DOS pauses before selecting the default. If you specify 0, DOS does not pause.
text	Specifies text to display for a CHOICE command

Example

The following batch file segment displays a menu listing A, B, and C options and asks the user for a choice:

```
@ECHO OFF
CLS
ECHO.
ECHO A     Windows 3.1
ECHO B     MS-DOS 6.0
ECHO C     Video Poker
ECHO.
CHOICE /c:abc Choose an option:
IF ERRORLEVEL 1 GOTO WINDOWS
IF ERRORLEVEL 2 GOTO REGULAR
IF ERRORLEVEL 3 GOTO POKER
:WINDOWS
```

```
WIN/S
GOTO END
:REGULAR
CLS
GOTO END
:POKER
VPOKER
GOTO END
:END
CLS
```

ECHO

Displays a message and either permits or inhibits the display of batch commands and messages by other batch subcommands as MS-DOS executes these subcommands. (See also **REM**.)

Syntax

To display a message, use the following syntax:

ECHO message

message is the text of the message to be displayed on-screen.

To display a blank line separating more than one *message*, use the following syntax:

ECHO.

To turn off the display of commands and messages by other batch commands, use the following syntax:

ECHO OFF

To turn on the display of commands and messages, use the following syntax:

ECHO ON

To see the status of ECHO, use the following syntax:

ECHO

Example

The following example uses the ECHO command to display messages:

```
ECHO OFF
ECHO To run this program, make sure
ECHO the disk containing BASICA is
ECHO in drive A and the disk labeled
ECHO CONTRACTS is in drive B.
ECHO.
ECHO (If you need to exit at this time,
ECHO hold down the Ctrl key and press
ECHO the Break key. When the system
ECHO asks you whether you want to
ECHO "Terminate batch job (Y/N)?"
ECHO press Y. The batch file will stop.)
```

The first command, ECHO OFF, is the "noise suppressor." ECHO OFF suppresses the *echoing* (displaying) of any batch commands on-screen as these commands are executed. However, ECHO OFF does not turn off messages displayed by another ECHO command. Running the preceding batch file produces the following display:

```
C>ECHO OFF
To run this program, make sure
the disk containing BASICA is
in drive A and the disk labeled
CONTRACTS is in drive B.

(If you need to exit at this time,
hold down the Ctrl key and press
the Break key. When the system
asks you whether you want to
"Terminate batch job (Y/N)?"
press Y. The batch file will stop.)
```

Notes

The ECHO message is not the same as the REM message. DOS does not display the message on the line with the REM subcommand if ECHO is off.

You can suppress the display of a single batch file line by using @ as the first character in a line. If you type @ECHO OFF, DOS does not display the ECHO OFF command on-screen. When you suppress ECHO in a batch file, you must reissue ECHO ON or exit a batch file to activate ECHO. If ECHO is turned off with ECHO OFF, and a second batch file is called, ECHO remains off.

To suppress the output of a command, use I/O redirection to the null device (NUL). For example, to suppress the file or files copied message when you are using COPY, type COPY file1.ext file2.ext >NUL. DOS sends the command's output to the null device and does not display the output on-screen.

FOR..IN..DO

Repeats processing of an MS-DOS command.

Syntax

FOR %%variable IN (set) DO command

variable is a single letter. **set** is one or more words or file specifications. The file specification is in the form *d:path***filename**.*ext*. You can use wild cards. **command** is the MS-DOS command to be performed for each word or file in the set.

Rules

You can use more than one word or a full file specification in the **set**. Separate words or file specifications with spaces or commas.

%%**variable** becomes each literal word or full file specification in the set. If you use wild cards, FOR..IN..DO executes once for each file that matches the wild-card file specification.

You can use path names.

You cannot nest FOR..IN..DO subcommands (put two of these subcommands on the same line). You can use other batch subcommands with FOR..IN..DO.

Example

This example uses FOR..IN..DO in a batch file called FORMAT.BAT that permits you to format only drive A: or drive B:.

```
ECHO OFF
IF %1. == . GOTO NONE
FOR %%a IN (a:, A:, b:, B:) DO IF %1 ==
     %%a GOTO FORMAT
ECHO You don't really mean to format %1,
     do you?
GOTO END
:NONE
ECHO You did not specify the drive (B), e.g.
     FORMAT B:
ECHO Please try the command again.
GOTO END
:FORMAT
XFORMAT   %1
:END
```

This batch file first tests for an empty parameter %1 because MS-DOS gives errors when testing anything against an empty string. The next command tests whether the designated disk drive is A or B, in both upper- and lowercase versions. If the letters match, processing jumps to where the file invokes the FORMAT command. If no match is found, processing drops to an error message and then jumps to END.

Note

set can contain literal words, separated by spaces. **set** replaces **%%variable** when the command executes. You can use FOR..IN..DO from the DOS command line with the following syntax:

FOR **%%variable** IN (set) DO command

GOTO

Transfers control to the line following the label in the batch file and continues batch file execution from that line.

Syntax

GOTO label

label is the name used for one or more characters, preceded by a colon. Only the first eight characters of the label name are significant.

Rules

The label must be the first item on a line in a batch file and must start with a colon (:).

DOS never executes a **label**. MS-DOS uses the label only as the jump-to marker for the GOTO subcommand.

If you issue a GOTO command with a nonexistent label, MS-DOS issues an error message and stops processing the batch file.

Example

This sample batch file uses GOTO and a label:

```
:START
DIR B:
PAUSE
GOTO START
```

As the first character in the line, the colon designates that the name START is a label. When this batch file is run, MS-DOS displays a list of the files on drive B and pauses. The final line directs MS-DOS to go to the :START line and execute the batch file again.

This batch file continues perpetually until you press Ctrl-Break or Ctrl-C to stop the action. (Unless it is absolutely necessary, do not use Ctrl-Break to stop a batch-file execution.)

IF

Permits conditional execution of an MS-DOS command.

Syntax

IF *NOT* condition command

NOT tests for the opposite of the **condition** (executes the command if the condition is false). **condition** is what is being tested and can be one of the following:

- **ERRORLEVEL number.** MS-DOS tests the exit code (0 to 255) of the program. If the exit code is greater than or equal to the number, the condition is true.

- **string1 == string2.** MS-DOS tests whether these two alphanumeric strings are identical.

- **EXIST** *d:path***filename**.*ext.* MS-DOS tests whether the file *d:path***filename**.*ext* is in the specified drive or path (if you specify a drive name or path name), or is on the current disk drive and directory.

command is any valid MS-DOS command or batch subcommand except another IF statement. You cannot put two or more IF subcommands on the same line.

Rules

The only MS-DOS programs that leave exit codes are BACKUP, DISKCOMP, DISKCOPY, FORMAT,

GRAFTABL, KEYB, REPLACE, RESTORE, SETVER, and XCOPY. Using an **ERRORLEVEL** condition with a program that does not leave an exit code is meaningless.

For **string1 == string2**, MS-DOS makes a literal, character-by-character comparison of the two strings. DOS bases the comparison on the ASCII character set and distinguishes between upper- and lowercase letters.

When you use **string1 == string2** with the parameter markers (%0 to %9), neither string may be null. If either string is null, MS-DOS displays a Syntax error message and aborts the batch file.

Examples

The batch file, MOVE.BAT, copies and deletes files, and uses IF to eliminate the potential disaster that may result from mistyping or omitting the directory name.

```
ECHO OFF
CLS
IF NOT EXIST C:\%1 GOTO ERROR1
COPY C:\%1 C:\%2 /V
IF NOT EXIST C:\%2\%1 GOTO ERROR2 ERASE
C:\%1
GOTO EXIT
:ERROR1
ECHO The file (%1) does not exist...
GOTO EXIT
:ERROR2
ECHO The copy of C:\%1 to C:\%2 was
unsuccessful!
ECHO C:\%1 was not erased.
:EXIT
```

This batch file tests whether the new file exists and is copied successfully. You combine C:\ with %1, the file name, and %2, which is the subdirectory that will hold the copied file. The result is a complete file name (C:\%2\%1), which is used in the test for existence. If the file exists, the COPY command was probably successful. If, however, anything is wrong, the batch file does not erase the original. This line is the "safety play." It does nothing destructive in case something has failed. When you create batch files, take the approach that everything must be right before any files are destroyed.

This next example illustrates the string-comparison option of IF. The example creates a special batch file called FMAT.BAT to enable you to format a 720K floppy disk in a 1.44M drive. Suppose that drive A is your 1.44M drive, and FORMAT.COM resides in the directory C:\DOS. Now create the following batch file and call it FMAT.BAT:

```
@ECHO OFF
IF %1. == . GOTO F144
IF %1. == 720. GOTO F720
GOTO END
:F144
ECHO Formatting drive A as a 1.44M floppy
disk.
C:\DOS\FORMAT A:
GOTO END
:F720
ECHO Formatting drive A as a 720K floppy
disk.
C:\DOS\FORMAT A: /F:720
:END
```

In this batch file, the IF subcommand is used to test for the equivalence of two strings. Remember that strings are defined as sets of any characters of any length. The assumption is that you do not give a parameter (you only type FMAT), so DOS formats the disk in drive A as the default 1.44M floppy disk. However, if the parameter is 720 (you type FMAT 720), DOS formats the floppy disk in drive A as a 720K floppy disk.

The first test was for an empty parameter. If the parameter is nonexistent, then DOS executes the GOTO F144 command. If the first parameter is not empty, however, then a test is made to see if the parameter is equal to 720. If %1 does equal 720, then DOS performs GOTO F720.

PAUSE

Suspends batch file processing until the user presses a key, and optionally displays a user's message.

Syntax

PAUSE *message*

message is a string of up to 121 characters.

Rules

Regardless of ECHO's setting, MS-DOS displays Strike a key when ready....

MS-DOS suspends the processing of the batch file until you press a key. Afterward, MS-DOS continues processing the batch file's lines. To end a batch file's processing, press Ctrl-Break or Ctrl-C.

Examples

Because the Strike any key when ready... message of PAUSE always shows on-screen, you can phrase your batch file message to take advantage of this line. For example, you can use these lines:

```
ECHO OFF
CLS
ECHO Place the proper disk into drive A,
ECHO and when the message appears,
ECHO press Enter to continue
ECHO or press Ctrl-Break
ECHO and then Y to stop the file, or
PAUSE
```

This set of lines yields the following screen:

```
Place the proper disk into drive A,
and when the message appears,
press Enter to continue
or press Ctrl-Break
and then Y to stop the file, or
Strike a key when ready ...
```

Adding one of the following two lines to this batch file before the PAUSE command makes the text much cleaner on-screen:

    ECHO . . . .

    ECHO.

The first line draws a dotted line to separate the message you create with ECHO commands in the batch file from the message that the PAUSE command gives.

You can create the second line by typing ECHO and a period with no space in between them. This key combination echoes back a blank line.

REM

Displays a message within the batch file.

Syntax

    REM message

message is a string of up to 123 characters.

Example

This example shows the beginning of a sample batch file with REM commands:

    REM To run this program, make sure
    REM the disk containing BASICA is in
    REM drive A and the disk labeled

CONTRACTS
REM is in drive B.
REM . . . .
REM (If you need to exit at this time,
REM hold down the REM Ctrl key and
REM press the Break key. When the system
REM asks you whether you want to
REM "Terminate batch job (Y/N)?"
REM press Y. The batch file will stop.)

When this batch file runs, MS-DOS displays the word REM followed by each remark line on-screen. MS-DOS does not execute anything on the line. If you want your messages to be clearer, use the batch subcommand ECHO.

Both ECHO and REM statements are useful in a batch file. With ECHO OFF, REM protects comments you want to remain in the batch file but do not want to appear on-screen, and ECHO displays messages on-screen. REM comments can serve as documentation when you or others want to change the file later, and ECHO messages can provide on-screen guidance. With ECHO ON, ECHO statements appear twice, and REM statements appear once.

SHIFT

Shifts the parameters given on the command line one position to the left when you invoke the batch file.

Syntax

SHIFT

Rules

When you use SHIFT, MS-DOS discards the former first parameter.

When you write a batch file to execute a command that works in pairs, such as RENAME, include two SHIFT commands instead of one. Each SHIFT command is an executable MS-DOS command.

Example

Use SHIFT when you are handling an undetermined number of similar parameters. For instance, you can take a file called MOVE.BAT (one that moves files to a predetermined subdirectory) and generalize it so that it can move any number of files.

```
ECHO OFF
CLS
:START
IF NOT EXIST C:\%1 GOTO ERROR1
COPY C:\%1 C:\SUBDIR1 /V
ERASE C:\%1
SHIFT
IF %1. == . GOTO EXIT
GOTO START
GOTO EXIT
:ERROR1
ECHO The file (%1) does not exist...
:EXIT
```

To move any number of files, you can enter the following command:

MOVE COMP.COM ABACUS.EXE

SLIDE.EXE LINK.EXE ABSCOND.COM

MOVE.BAT substitutes the first file (COMP.COM) for %1, processes the file, and shifts the parameters so that the second file (ABACUS.EXE) now becomes %1, and so on.

CONFIG.SYS COMMANDS

CONFIG.SYS commands define to the operating system how your system will be configured. They provide a method to load device drivers (such as those for printers, keyboard, and memory), set the number of open files and buffers to use, and install some memory-resident programs into HMA or upper memory blocks, for example.

BREAK

(Ctrl-Break Checking)   Internal

When on, causes MS-DOS to look for a Ctrl-Break or a Ctrl-C to stop a program.

Syntax

To turn on BREAK, use the following syntax:

BREAK=ON

To turn off BREAK, use the following syntax:

BREAK=OFF

BUFFERS

(Set number of disk buffers)   Internal

Sets the number of disk buffers set aside by MS-DOS in memory.

Syntax

BUFFERS=*nn,c*

nn is the number of buffers to set, from 1 to 99. The default is 8. *c* is the number of sectors, from 0 to 8, that DOS can read or write to at a time. The default is 0.

COMMAND

(Start new instance of Command Interpreter) External

Invokes a new copy of the MS-DOS command interpreter. (See also **SHELL**.)

Syntax

> COMMAND=*d:path***filename.***ext d:path*
> */E:nnnn /C string /P /MSG*

d: is the name of the drive where MS-DOS can find the command processor. *path* is the MS-DOS path to the command processor. **filename.***ext* is the file name and optional extension of the command processor.

Switches

/E:nnnn	Tells MS-DOS to set a command interpreter environment size. *nnnn* specifies the size of the environment in bytes. Valid environment values range from 160 to 32,768 bytes.
/C string	Tells the command interpreter to execute any commands following the */C* and then return to the original command interpreter
/P	Instructs MS-DOS to make the specified command interpreter the permanent command shell
/MSG	Instructs MS-DOS to load its error messages into conventional memory. This switch requires that you use the */P* switch also.

COUNTRY

(Set country-dependent information)   Internal

Instructs MS-DOS to modify the input and display of date, time, and field divider information.

Syntax

COUNTRY=nnn,mmm,*d:path*filenamef.extf

nnn is the country code. **mmm** is the code page. *d:path* is the drive and directory that contain **filenamef.extf**. **filenamef.extf** is the file that contains the country information (COUNTRY.SYS).

DEVICE

(Set device driver)   Internal

Instructs MS-DOS to load, link, and use a special device driver.

Syntax

DEVICE=*d:path*filename.*ext options*

d: is the name of the drive on which MS-DOS can find the device driver. *path* is the MS-DOS path to the device driver. **filename.***ext* is the root file name and optional extension of the device driver. *options* are any command-line switches the device driver you are loading may require.

DEVICEHIGH   **6**

(Load device driver into upper memory)   Internal

Instructs MS-DOS to load, link, and use a special
device driver in the reserved (upper) memory of an
80386 or greater computer.

Syntax

> DEVICEHIGH *dd:pathd*\filenamed.extd
> */L:region#,minsize# /S options*

dd:pathd\ is the disk drive and path on which
the device driver is located. **filenamed.extd** is the
actual file name and extension of the device driver.
options are any command-line switches the device
driver you are loading may require.

Switches

/L:region#,minsize#   Tells DOS to load the
device driver in a specified
region (#) and defines the
minimum memory size for
that region

/S   Tells DOS to shrink, to the
smallest size possible, the
upper memory block into
which a device driver is
loading. Use this switch
only with MEMMAKER and
the */L* switch.

DOS

(Load DOS into high memory)   Internal

Loads DOS into the high memory area of the computer or controls a link between conventional

memory and reserved memory. This command
requires an 80286 computer or greater with extended memory.

Syntax

DOS=HIGH | LOW, UMB | NOUMB

HIGH places a portion of DOS into the high memory
area. **LOW** is the default setting, and causes DOS to
reside entirely in conventional memory.

UMB establishes and maintains a link between
conventional memory and the upper memory blocks
in reserved memory for 80386 and 80486 computers.
NOUMB is the default setting, which disconnects a
link between conventional memory and the upper
memory blocks in reserved memory for 80386 or
greater computers.

Examples

To load DOS into high memory, type DOS=HIGH.

To load DOS in high memory and activate upper
memory blocks on an 80386 or greater computer,
type DOS=HIGH, UMB.

DRIVPARM

(Define block device)　　　　　　　**Internal**

Defines or changes the parameters of a block device
such as a disk drive.

Syntax

DRIVPARM=/D:num /C /F:type /H:hds /I /N
/S:sec /T:trk

Switches

/C	Causes the drive to support *change-line*, meaning that the drive has sensor support to determine when the drive door is open. When the drive door is open, the drive is sensed as empty.
/D:num	Specifies the drive number, num, ranging from 0 to 255, where drive A=0, drive B=1, drive C=2, and so on
/F:type	Determines the type of drive. Type 2 is the default if you do not specify /F. *type* is one of the following:

Type	Drive specification
0	160K/320K/180K/360K
1	1.2M
2	720K
5	Hard disk
6	Tape drive
7	1.44M
8	Read/write optical disk
9	2.88M

/H:hds	Specifies the total number of drive heads, where *hds* is a number from 1 to 99. The default for *hds* is 2.
/I	Use this switch if you have a 3 1/2-inch drive connected internally to your floppy drive controller, but your ROM BIOS does not support a 3 1/2-inch drive
/N	Specifies that your drive or other block device is not removable

| /S:sec | Specifies the total number of sectors per side on the drive. *sec* can be a number from 1 to 999. |
| /T:trk | Specifies the number of tracks per side of a disk or the total number of tracks per tape. *trk* can be a number from 1 to 99. |

FCBS

(Set Control Blocks)   **Internal**

Specifies the number of MS-DOS File Control Blocks that can be open concurrently.

Syntax

FCBS=maxopen

maxopen is the number of FCBs that can be open at any given time. The default is 4. The allowable range is 1 to 255.

FILES

(Set maximum open files)   **Internal**

Specifies the number of file handles that may be open at any given time.

Syntax

FILES=nnn

nnn is the number of file handles that may be open at any given time. The default is 8. Valid file handles may be 8 to 255.

HIMEM.SYS

6

(Extended memory manager) **External**

Manages the high memory area (HMA) where device drivers and TSR programs are loaded.

Syntax

DEVICE=*dc:pathc*\HIMEM.SYS /
A20CONTROL:ON|OFF /CPUCLOCK:ON|OFF
/EISA /HMAMIN=x /INT15=xxxx
/NUMHANDLES=x /MACHINE:xxxx
/SHADOWRAM:ON|OFF /VERBOSE

Switches

/A20CONTROL:ON|OFF	Specifies whether HIMEM.SYS should take control of the A20 handler. The default is ON.
/CPUCLOCK:ON|OFF	Tells HIMEM.SYS how to work with the clock in your computer. The default is OFF.
/EISA	Specifies that HIMEM.SYS should take control of all extended memory on EISA machines with 16M of RAM or more
/HMAMIN=x	Specifies the largest block of HMA memory that an application can require. Valid values are 0 to 63. The default is 0.
/INT15=xxxx	Reserves a specified amount of extended memory for older applications that use

DOS Interrupt 15h for extended memory allocation rather than using XMS. Valid values range from 64 to 65535 K. The default is 0.

/NUMHANDLES=x

Specifies how many EMB handles HIMEM.SYS can use at one time. Valid values are 1 to 128. The default is 32.

/MACHINE:xxxx

Specifies the type of computer you are using if HIMEM.SYS is unable to determine it. Refer to your DOS reference manual for specific machine types.

/SHADOWRAM:ON|OFF

Tells HIMEM.SYS whether to disable shadow RAM. On some systems, HIMEM.SYS attempts to disable shadow RAM on computers with less than 2M of RAM.

/VERBOSE or /V

Provides a status report when loading HIMEM.SYS

Note

You must load HIMEM.SYS before the DOS=HIGH command in your CONFIG.SYS.

INSTALL

(Load TSR into memory)   **Internal**

Starts a program from CONFIG.SYS. Valid programs to start with INSTALL are FASTOPEN, KEYB,

NLSFUNC, SHARE, and other programs that remain in the computer's random-access memory (RAM).

Syntax

INSTALL=*dc:pathc*filename.ext *options*

filename.ext is the name of the file, which may be FASTOPEN.EXE, KEYB.EXE, NLSFUNC.EXE, SHARE.EXE, and other valid TSR programs. *options* are any parameters the filename.ext command requires.

Note

INSTALL is not generally used with TSR programs requiring activation by hot keys (SideKick, for example).

LASTDRIVE

(Specify last system drive)   Internal

Sets the last valid drive letter acceptable to MS-DOS.

Syntax

LASTDRIVE=x

x is the alphabetical character for the highest system drive. You can use single letters from A to Z.

Note

You can only SUBST drives up to the preset drive letter set with the LASTDRIVE line in your CONFIG.SYS file.

RAMDRIVE.SYS

(Emulate disk drive in RAM) External

Simulates a physical disk drive using RAM.

Syntax

DEVICE=*dc:pathc*\RAMDRIVE.SYS disksize
sectorsize entries /E /A

disksize specifies how large you want the RAMDISK
to be in kilobytes. The default is 64K. If you use
disksize, you should use **sectorsize** as well.
sectorsize specifies how large the sectorsize
should be in bytes, from 128 to 512 bytes. If you use
sectorsize, you must use **disksize** as well. **entries**
specifies how many files can be created in the root
directory of the RAMDISK, from 2 to 1,024 entries.
The default is 64. If you use **entries**, you must also
use **disksize** and **sectorsize**.

Switches

/E   Specifies that DOS creates the
          RAMDISK in extended memory

/A   Specifies that DOS creates the
          RAMDISK in expanded
          memory

REM

(Remark) Internal

Places remarks or hidden statements in the
CONFIG.SYS file.

Syntax

> REM remark

remark is any text that you want to insert into the
CONFIG.SYS file.

SETVER

(Emulate previous DOS versions)   External

Sets a specific DOS version to be emulated with a
program file.

Syntax

> DEVICE=*dc:pathc*\SETVER.EXE

SHELL

(Specify command processor)   Internal

Specifies the default MS-DOS command processor
(command interpreter). (See also **COMMAND** and
COMSPEC.)

Syntax

> SHELL=d:path\filename.*ext* /E:*nnnn* /P /MSG

d: is the name of the drive that contains the command processor. **path** is the MS-DOS path to the
command processor. **filename**.*ext* is the file name
and optional extension of the command processor.

Switches

> /E:*nnnn*   Sets a command interpreter
>   environment size. *nnnn*
>   specifies the size of the

	environment in bytes. Valid environment values range from 160 to 32,768 bytes.
/P	Makes the specified command interpreter the permanent command shell
/MSG	Loads DOS error messages into conventional memory. To use this switch, you must also use the /P switch.

Example

To tell MS-DOS you want to use the file COMMAND.COM located in your DOS directory with an environment size of 512 bytes as your permanent shell, type the following statement in your CONFIG.SYS: SHELL=C:\DOS\COMMAND.COM C:\DOS /E:512 /P.

STACKS

(Allocate interrupt storage)   **Internal**

Allots memory storage to accommodate hardware interrupts.

Syntax

STACKS=n,m

n is the number of allotted stacks. The default for computers using the 8088/8086 microprocessor is 0, whereas the default for those computers using the 80286, 80386sx, and 80386 is 9. **m** is the size in bytes of each stack. The default for computers using the 8088/8086 microprocessor is 0, whereas the default for those computers using the 80286, 80386sx, and 80386 is 128.

MULTICONFIG

MULTICONFIG designs a multiple configuration selection menu from which you can choose a specific configuration to boot your computer.

Syntax

You can design menus in your CONFIG.SYS file by using the following commands: [Include], [Menu], [Menucolor], [Menudefault], [Menuitem], [Numlock], [Submenu].

To tell DOS that a MultiConfig environment exists, begin by defining a [Menu] at the beginning of your CONFIG.SYS file. The [Menu] block tells DOS what to display at the time your computer boots, and what configurations you have to choose from before the system completes the boot process.

[Include] lets you specify commands for a particular menu choice and include configuration commands from another menu choice. Use the syntax Include=menuitem within a block configuration to include that menu item's configuration commands.

Each configuration, called a configuration block, begins with a block header [Menuitem] and lists the commands DOS carries out based on your choice from the [Menu] presented at boot time.

You can establish a default and timeout value by using the block heading [Menudefault], as shown in the following example:

[Menudefault]=*block heading,value*

The setting *block heading* refers to a specific [Menuitem] established in the [Menu] block. The *value* setting is a timeout value ranging from 0 to 90 seconds. If you set the *value* to zero, DOS chooses the default, bypassing the menu entirely.

You can use a special configuration block, [Common], to tell DOS which commands to carry out that are common to all menu choices.

Screen colors can be set either as a common environment for all users, or they can be set for each user. Refer to your MS-DOS Reference Manual for more information on setting screen colors in menu configurations.

Examples

In the following example, three separate menu items are configured for three different individuals. The [menuitem] block lists the options for each individual. In addition, [common] defines system configuration items common to all users. The [submenu] option automatically invokes hard disk maintenance utilities:

```
[Menudefault]=Greg,10

[Menu]
menuitem=Greg
menuitem=Debbie
menuitem=Babette
submenu Maintenance, Set Up For System
Maintenance

[Common]
device=c:\dos\himem.sys
device=c:\mouse\mouse.sys

[Greg]
device=c:\dos\emm386.exe ram x=a000-cfff
x=d800-dfff
dos=high
files=50
buffers=10
device=c:\scan\hpscannr.sys
device=c:\ad\addrvr.sys
device=c:\dos\dispps.exe
```

```
[Debbie]
device=c:\dos\emm386.exe ram x=a000-cfff
x=d800-dfff
dos=high
files=70
buffers=30
device=c:\dos\connect.sys

[Babette]
device=c:\dos\emm386.exe ram x=a000-cfff
x=d800-dfff
files=50
buffers=20

[Maintenance]
files=60
buffers=20
[Common]
```

When DOS recognizes that multiple configurations
have been established, an environment variable (see
PATH and **COMMAND** for additional environment
variable information) called *CONFIG* is then in
effect. Combining this environment variable with
batch file execution in your AUTOEXEC.BAT file
gives you a powerful capability to precisely define
what program or programs are run for each individual [Menuitem].

For example, if Greg has selected his own [Menu]
choice when the system boots, the environment
variable *CONFIG* holds the menu choice "Greg".
If you wanted Greg to be able to boot directly into
Windows, you could set up your AUTOEXEC.BAT file
to test for the *CONFIG* environment variable and
then act on the variable's contents, as shown in the
following example:

```
@ECHO OFF
CLS
PATH C:\DOS;C:\WINDOWS;C:\UTILS;
IF "%CONFIG%"=="GREG" GOTO GREG
IF "%CONFIG%"=="DEBBIE" GOTO DEBBIE
```

```
IF "%CONFIG"%=="BABETTE" GOTO BABETTE
IF "%CONFIG"%=="MAINTENANCE" GOTO
MAINTENANCE
:GREG
WIN /3
GOTO END
:DEBBIE
C:\WORD\WORD
GOTO END
:BABETTE
C:\QUICKEN\QB
GOTO END
:MAINTENANCE
C:\PCTOOLS\COMPRESS
GOTO END
:END
CLS
```

Notes

DOS allows up to nine [Menu] items per menu. Use the [Submenu] option if you need more menu items.

You can use up to 70 characters to title a [Menuitem] block on your menu. Do not use forward and backward slashes, semicolons, equal signs, or square brackets in the [Menuitem] names.

Place the [Common] configuration commands at the top of your CONFIG.SYS file and define a second, empty [Common] block header at the bottom of your CONFIG.SYS to prevent problems when installing software, as shown in the previous example. DOS processes commands within [Common] blocks in order, from the top to the bottom of the CONFIG.SYS file.

NUMLOCK ON and NUMLOCK OFF only function in MULTICONFIG blocks; they do not function at the DOS command line.

DOS EDIT

EDIT is a full-screen editor. Using EDIT is similar to using a word processor. With EDIT's menu system, you easily can edit, cut and paste text, search and replace text, print, and save a file.

Although you can create small files faster with COPY CON, you cannot edit a COPY CON file as you are creating it. EDIT, however, is especially useful for involved programming and text entry.

Use EDIT to create, edit, and save batch, text, and other ASCII files. You also use EDIT to create source files for C, assembly language, or any programming language. You also can create control codes and special graphic characters that you want to use in a file.

Note that EDIT is a separate program with its own commands and menus. EDIT must be running before you can use its commands and menus. The following section explains how to start the EDIT program. This section explains how to create a file, enter text, and save the file.

Starting EDIT

1. Type EDIT. Because EDIT is an external program, you may need to precede the command with a drive name and path.

2. Optionally, type a space and the drive name, path, and name of the file you want to create or edit. Do not use wild cards (* or ?).

3. You can use any of EDIT's switches to alter the appearance of EDIT on-screen:

   /B   Places EDIT in black-and-white
                    screen colors

/G	Quickly writes to a CGA monitor (may cause "snow" on some monitors)
/H	Displays text in the maximum lines that your screen supports (43 for EGA and 50 for VGA)
/NOHI	Uses reverse video rather than high-intensity characters (for LCD screens)

4. Press Enter.

5. Choose EDIT's menus at the top of the screen. You can access these menus by pressing Alt and the highlighted letter of the menu name, or by selecting the menu with the mouse.

6. You can use any of EDIT's menu commands to edit the file, or use the File menu to Open, Save, or Print a file.

7. Press PgUp, PgDn, Home, End, and the cursor-movement keys to move the cursor.

8. From the File menu, select Save and then select Exit to save the file and exit EDIT. If you are creating a new file, EDIT prompts you for a file name. If you edit a file without saving, you are asked whether you want to save the file. Select Yes to save the file, No if you do not want to save changes, or Cancel to continue editing the file.

Using EDIT Commands

Command	Description
Clear(Edit menu)	Removes the high-lighted text from the file

continues

Command	Description
Copy(Edit menu)	Copies the highlighted text into temporary memory without removing the highlighted text
Cut(Edit menu)	Removes the highlighted text from the file, but keeps the last text you cut in temporary memory
Display...(Options menu)	Changes the colors of the screen
Exit(File menu)	Exits EDIT and provides you with the option to save the file if it has not been saved
Find...(Search menu)	Locates text in the file
Help Path(Options menu)	Specifies the location of the EDIT help file
New(File menu)	Clears the current file, if any, and enables you to save the old file and then create a new file
Open...(File menu)	Loads a file from disk into memory for editing
Paste(Edit menu)	Places cut or copied text from the temporary memory into the current file
Print...(File menu)	Prints the current file in memory to the printer

Command	Description
Save(File menu)	Saves the current file to disk by the same name as was retrieved or enables you to select a name if the file is new
Save as...(File menu)	Saves the current file in memory by a different name
Repeat Last Find (Search menu)	Repeats the most recent search
Replace...(Search menu)	Locates text in the file and replaces it with other text.

MS-DOS MESSAGES

MS-DOS messages fall into two groups: *general* MS-DOS messages and MS-DOS *device error* messages. For your version of MS-DOS, the actual wording of error messages may differ from those shown here. If you get a message that you cannot locate in this guide, refer to your computer's MS-DOS manual.

General MS-DOS Messages

The following messages may appear when you start MS-DOS or use your computer. Messages that usually appear when you start MS-DOS are marked (start-up). Most start-up errors mean that MS-DOS did not start and you must reboot the system. Most of the other error messages mean that MS-DOS terminated (aborted) the program and returned to the system prompt (A>). The messages are listed in alphabetical order for easy reference.

`Bad command or filename`

ERROR: The name you entered is not valid for invoking a command, program, or batch file. You most frequently see this message for the following reasons:

- You misspelled a name.

- You omitted a needed disk drive or path name.

- You gave the parameters without the command name, such as typing myfile instead of ws myfile (omitting the ws for WordStar).

Check the spelling on the command line. Make sure that the command, program, or batch file is in the location specified (disk drive and directory path). Then try the command again.

`Bad or missing Command Interpreter`

ERROR (start-up): MS-DOS cannot find the command interpreter, normally COMMAND.COM. MS-DOS does not start.

If you are starting MS-DOS, this message means COMMAND.COM is not on the boot disk or that a version of COMMAND.COM from a previous MS-DOS version is on the disk. If you have used the SHELL directive of CONFIG.SYS, the message means that it is improperly phrased or that COMMAND.COM is not where you specified. Place another floppy disk that contains the operating system in the floppy disk drive and then reset the system. After MS-DOS has started, copy COMMAND.COM to the original start-up disk so that you can boot from that disk.

If resetting the system does not solve the problem, use a copy of your MS-DOS boot floppy disk to restart the computer. Copy COMMAND.COM from this floppy disk to the offending disk.

`Bad or missing filename`

WARNING (start-up): MS-DOS was requested to load a device driver that it cannot locate, an error occurs when the device driver loads, or a break address for the device driver is out of bounds for the size of RAM memory that the computer is using. MS-DOS continues its boot but does not use the device driver *filename*. *filename* is the name of the file that DOS cannot find.

If MS-DOS loads, check your CONFIG.SYS file for the line DEVICE=*filename*. Make sure the line is spelled correctly and the device driver is where you specified. If this line is correct, reboot the system. If the message appears again, copy the file from its original floppy disk to the boot floppy disk and try booting MS-DOS again. If the error persists, the device driver is bad. Contact the dealer or publisher who sold it to you.

Batch file missing

ERROR: MS-DOS cannot find the batch file it is processing. The batch file may have been erased or renamed. MS-DOS aborts the processing of the batch file.

If you renamed the batch file, rename it again, using the original name. If required, edit the batch file to ensure that the file name does not get changed again. If the file was erased, re-create the batch file from its backup file, if possible. Edit the file to ensure that the batch file does not erase itself.

Cannot load COMMAND, system halted

ERROR: MS-DOS attempts to reload COMMAND.COM, but the area where MS-DOS keeps track of available and used memory is destroyed, or DOS does not find the command processor in the directory specified by the COMSPEC= entry. The system halts.

This message indicates either that COMMAND.COM was erased from the disk and directory you used when starting MS-DOS, or that the COMSPEC= entry in the environment was changed. Restart MS-DOS. If it does not start, the copy of COMMAND.COM was erased. Restart MS-DOS from the original master floppy disks and copy COMMAND.COM to your other disk.

`Cannot start COMMAND, exiting`

ERROR: MS-DOS cannot load an additional copy of COMMAND.COM as directed.

Either your CONFIG.SYS FILES= command is set too low, or you do not have enough free memory for another copy of COMMAND.COM. If your system has 256K or more and FILES is less than 10, edit the CONFIG.SYS file on your start-up floppy disk and use FILES = 15 or FILES = 20, then reboot.

If the problem occurs again, you do not have enough memory in your computer or you have too many resident or background programs competing for memory space. Restart MS-DOS and load only essential resident or background programs. If necessary, eliminate unneeded device drivers or RAM disk software. Another alternative is to increase the amount of RAM memory in your system.

`Current drive is no longer valid`

WARNING: You set the system prompt to PROMPT $p. At the system level, MS-DOS attempts to read the current directory for the disk drive and finds that the drive is no longer valid.

If the current disk drive is set for a floppy disk, this warning appears when you do not have a floppy disk in the disk drive. MS-DOS reports a `Drive not ready` error. Enter the F to fail or I to ignore the error. Then insert a floppy disk into the disk drive.

The invalid drive error can also occur if you have a current networked or SUBST disk drive that has been deleted or disconnected. Change the current disk to a valid disk drive.

`Directory already exists`

ERROR: Either you or a program attempts to create a directory, and a directory or a file by the same name already exists.

Use the DIR command on the disk. Make sure no file or directory exists with the same name. If adding the directory to the root directory, remove or move (copy, then erase) any unneeded files or directories.

Disk boot failure

ERROR (start-up): An error occurs when MS-DOS tries to load itself into memory. The floppy disk contains IO.SYS and MSDOS.SYS, but one of the two files cannot load. MS-DOS does not boot.

Try starting MS-DOS from the floppy disk again. If the error recurs, try booting MS-DOS from a floppy disk you know is good, such as a copy of your MS-DOS master floppy disk. If this action fails, you have a hardware disk drive problem. Contact your local dealer. If you can boot from a master MS-DOS floppy disk, however, use SYS to transfer DOS to the floppy disk causing the error.

Divide overflow

ERROR: A program attempts to divide by zero. MS-DOS aborts the program.

Either the program was incorrectly entered, or it contains a flaw in logic. With a well-written program, this error should never occur. If you wrote the program, correct the error and try the program again. If you purchased the program, report the problem to the dealer or publisher. This message also can appear when you are attempting to format a RAM disk. Make sure you are formatting the correct disk and try again.

Error in EXE file

ERROR: MS-DOS detects an error while attempting to load a program stored in an .EXE file.

The problem is in the relocation information MS-DOS needs to load the program. This problem can occur if the .EXE file has been altered in any way. Restart MS-DOS and try the program again, this time using a backup copy of the program. If the message reappears, the program is flawed. Try copying the

EXE file from an original disk. If the problem still exists, contact the manufacturer of the program.

Error loading operating system

ERROR (start-up): A disk error occurs while MS-DOS is loading itself from the hard disk. MS-DOS does not boot.

Restart the computer. If the error occurs after several tries, restart MS-DOS from the floppy disk drive. If the hard disk does not respond (that is, you cannot run DIR or CHKDSK without getting an error), you have a problem with the hard disk. Contact your local dealer. If the hard disk does respond, use the SYS command to put another copy of MS-DOS onto your hard disk. You may need to copy COMMAND.COM to the hard disk also.

EXEC failure

ERROR: MS-DOS encounters an error while reading a command or program from the disk, or the CONFIG.SYS FILES= command has too low a value.

Increase the number of FILES in the CONFIG.SYS file of your start-up disk to 15 or 20, and then restart MS-DOS. If the error recurs, you may have a problem with the disk. Use a backup copy of the program and try again. If the backup copy works, copy it over the offending copy of your start-up disk.

If an error occurs in the copying process, you have a flawed floppy disk or hard disk. If the problem is with a floppy disk, copy the files from the flawed floppy disk to another floppy disk and reformat or retire the original floppy disk. If the problem is with the hard disk, immediately back up your files and run RECOVER on the offending file. If the problem persists, your hard disk may have a hardware failure.

File allocation table bad, drive d Abort, Retry, Fail?

WARNING: MS-DOS encountered a problem in the File Allocation Table (FAT) of the disk in drive D.

Type **R** for Retry several times. If this does not solve the problem, use **A** for Abort. If you are using a floppy disk, attempt to copy all the files to another floppy disk and then reformat or retire the original floppy disk. If you are using a hard disk, back up all files on the disk and reformat the hard disk. The disk is unusable until reformatted.

File creation error

ERROR: Either a program or MS-DOS attempts to add a new file to the directory or to replace an existing file, but fails.

If the file already exists, use the ATTRIB command to check whether the file is marked as read-only. If the read-only flag is set and you want to change or erase the file, use ATTRIB to remove the read-only flag and then try again.

If the problem is not a read-only flag, run CHKDSK without the /F switch to determine whether the directory is full, the disk is full, or some other problem exists with the disk.

File not found

ERROR: MS-DOS cannot find the file you specified.

The file is not on the correct floppy disk or in the correct directory; or you misspelled the disk drive name, path name, or file name. Check these possibilities and try the command again.

Filename device driver cannot be initialized

WARNING (start-up): In CONFIG.SYS, either the parameters in the device driver *filename* are incorrect, or the DEVICE line is in error.

Check for incorrect parameters and for phrasing errors in the DEVICE line. Edit the DEVICE line in the CONFIG.SYS file, save the file, and restart MS-DOS.

`Incorrect MS-DOS version`

ERROR: The copy of the file holding the command you just entered is from a different version of MS-DOS.

Get a copy of the command from the appropriate version of MS-DOS (usually from your copy of the MS-DOS master floppy disk) and try the command again. If the disk or floppy disk you are using has been updated to hold new versions of the MS-DOS programs, copy those versions over the old ones.

If a utility gives you this error, then you may "trick" the utility into believing an older version of DOS is running. Use the SETVER command to enter a DOS version the utility should recognize.

`Insert disk with \COMMAND.COM in drive d`
`Press any key to continue`

INFORMATIONAL and WARNING: MS-DOS needs to reload COMMAND.COM but cannot find it on the start-up disk.

If you are using floppy disks, probably the floppy disk in drive A has been changed. Place a floppy disk containing a good copy of COMMAND.COM in drive A and press a key.

`Insert disk with batch file`
`Press any key to continue`

INFORMATIONAL: MS-DOS is attempting to execute the next command from a batch file, but the floppy disk containing the batch file is not in the disk drive.

Put the floppy disk containing the batch file into the disk drive and press a key to continue.

`Insert floppy disk for drive d and`
`strike any key when ready`

INFORMATIONAL: On a system with one floppy disk drive, either you or a program specify the tandem disk drive D (A or B). This drive is different from the current disk drive.

If the correct floppy disk is in the disk drive, press a key. Otherwise, put the correct floppy disk into the floppy disk drive and then press a key.

Insufficient disk space

WARNING or ERROR: The disk does not have enough free space to hold the file being written. All MS-DOS programs terminate when this problem occurs, but some non-DOS programs continue.

If you think the disk has enough room to hold this file, run CHKDSK to see whether there is a problem with the hard disk or floppy disk. Sometimes when you terminate programs early by pressing Ctrl-Break, MS-DOS is unable to do the necessary clean-up work, and disk space is temporarily trapped. CHKDSK can "free" these areas.

If you have run out of disk space, free some disk space or use a different floppy disk or hard disk. Try the command again.

Insufficient memory

ERROR: The computer does not have enough free RAM memory to execute the program or command.

If you loaded a resident program such as PRINT, GRAPHICS, MODE, or MIRROR, restart MS-DOS and try the command before loading any resident program. If this method fails, remove any unneeded device driver or RAM-disk software from the CONFIG.SYS file and restart MS-DOS again. If this action fails, your computer does not have enough memory to run this command. You must increase your RAM memory.

Intermediate file error during pipe

ERROR: MS-DOS is unable to create or write to one or both of the intermediate files it uses when piping (|) information between programs. The disk or root directory is full, or MS-DOS cannot locate the files.

The most frequent cause is a lack of disk space. Run the DIR command on the root directory of the current disk drive. Make sure you have enough free space and enough room in the root directory for two additional files. If you do not have enough room, make room on the disk by deleting, or copying and deleting, files. You may also copy the necessary files to a different floppy disk with sufficient room.

A program may be deleting files, including the temporary files MS-DOS uses. If this is the case, correct the program, contact the dealer or program publisher, or avoid using the program with piping.

Internal stack overflow System halted

ERROR: Your programs and MS-DOS exhaust the stack, the memory space that is reserved for temporary use.

This problem is usually caused by a rapid succession of hardware devices demanding attention (interrupts). To prevent this error from ever occurring, add the STACKS directive to your CONFIG.SYS file. If the directive is already in your CONFIG.SYS file, increase the number of stacks specified.

Invalid COMMAND.COM in drive d

WARNING: MS-DOS tries to reload from the disk in drive D and finds that it contains a different version of MS-DOS.

An on-screen message instructing you to insert a floppy disk with the correct version and press a key appears. Follow the directions given by the message. If you frequently use the floppy disk that was originally in the disk drive, copy the correct version of COMMAND.COM to that floppy disk.

Invalid COMMAND.COM, system halted

ERROR: MS-DOS cannot find COMMAND.COM on the hard disk. MS-DOS halts and must be restarted.

COMMAND.COM may have been erased, or the COMSPEC= setting in the environment may have been changed. Restart the computer from the hard disk. If you see a message that indicates COMMAND.COM is missing, that file was erased. Restart MS-DOS from a floppy disk and recopy COMMAND.COM to the root directory of the hard disk or to wherever your SHELL command directs, if you have used this command in your CONFIG.SYS file.

If you restart MS-DOS and this message appears later, a program or batch file is erasing COMMAND.COM or is altering the COMSPEC= parameter. If a batch file is erasing COMMAND.COM, edit the batch file. If a program is erasing COMMAND.COM, contact the dealer or publisher that sold you the program. If COMSPEC= is being altered, either edit the offending batch file or program, or place COMMAND.COM in the sub-directory expected by your program or batch file.

Invalid directory

ERROR: One of the following errors occurred:

- You specified a directory name that does not exist.

- You misspelled the directory name.

- The directory path is on a different disk.

- You forgot to give the path character (\) at the beginning of the name.

- You did not separate the directory names with the path character.

Check your directory names, ensure that the directories do exist, and try the command again.

Invalid disk change

WARNING: The floppy disk in the 720K, 1.2M, or 1.44M disk drive was changed while a program had open files to be written to the floppy disk.

The message Abort, Retry, Fail appears on-screen. Place the correct floppy disk in the disk drive and type R for Retry.

Invalid drive in search path

WARNING: A specification you gave to the PATH command has an invalid disk drive name, or a named disk drive is nonexistent or hidden temporarily by a SUBST or JOIN command.

Use PATH to check the paths you instructed MS-DOS to search. If you gave a nonexistent disk drive name, use the PATH command again and enter the correct search paths. If the problem is temporary because of a SUBST or JOIN command, you can again use PATH to enter the paths, but leave out or correct the wrong entry. Or you can just ignore the warning message.

Invalid drive specification

ERROR: This message occurs for the following reasons:

- You entered the name of an invalid or nonexistent disk drive as a parameter to a command.

- You specified the same disk drive for the source and destination, which is not permitted for the command.

- By not specifying a parameter, you have defaulted to the same source and destination disk drive.

Remember that certain MS-DOS commands (such as SUBST and JOIN) temporarily hide disk drive names while the command is in effect. Check the disk drive names. If the command is objecting to a missing parameter and defaulting to the wrong disk drive, explicitly name the correct disk drive.

Invalid drive specification
Specified drive does not exist
or is non-removable

ERROR: One of the following errors occurred:

- You specified the name of a nonexistent disk drive.

■ You named the hard disk drive when using commands for floppy disks only.

■ You did not specify a disk drive name and defaulted to the hard disk when using commands for floppy disks only.

■ You named or defaulted to a RAM-disk drive when using commands for a "real" floppy disk only.

Remember that certain MS-DOS commands (such as SUBST and JOIN) temporarily hide disk drive names while the command is in effect. Check the disk drive name you gave and try the command again.

Invalid environment size specified

WARNING: You have given the SHELL directive in CONFIG.SYS. The environment-size switch (/E:size) contains either non-numeric characters or a number that is less than 160 or greater than 32768.

If you are using the SHELL /E:size switch of MS-DOS V3.1, *size* is the number of 16-byte memory blocks, not the number of bytes.

Check the form of your CONFIG.SYS SHELL directive; the form needs to be exact. There must be a colon between /E and *size*; there must not be a comma or space between or within the /E: and the *size* characters; and the number in *size* should be greater than or equal to 160, but less than or equal to 32768.

Invalid partition table

ERROR (start-up): While you are attempting to start MS-DOS from the hard disk, MS-DOS detects a problem in the hard disk's partition information.

Restart MS-DOS from a floppy disk. Back up all files from the hard disk, if possible. Run FDISK to correct the problem. If you change the partition information, you must reformat the hard disk and restore all its files.

Invalid path

ERROR: One of the following errors has occurred to a path name you entered: the path name contains illegal characters; the name has more than 63 characters; one of the directory names within the path is misspelled or does not exist.

Check the spelling of the path name. If needed, run the DIR command on the disk and ensure that the directory you have specified does exist and that you have the correct path name. Be sure that the path name contains 63 characters or less. If necessary, change the current directory to a directory "closer" to the file and shorten the path name.

Invalid STACK parameter

WARNING (start-up): One of the following errors has occurred to the STACKS directive in your CONFIG.SYS file: a comma is missing between the number of stacks and the size of the stack; the number of stack frames is not in the range of 8 to 64; the stack size is not in the range of 32 to 512; you have omitted either the number of stack frames or the stack size; or either the stack frame or the stack size (but not both) is 0. MS-DOS continues to start but ignores the STACKS directive.

Check the STACKS directive in your CONFIG.SYS file. Edit and save the file, and restart MS-DOS.

Invalid switch character

WARNING: You have used VDISK.SYS in your CONFIG.SYS file. VDISK encounters a switch (/) but the character immediately following it is not an *E* for *extended memory*. MS-DOS loads VDISK and attempts to install VDISK in low (nonextended) memory.

Either you have misspelled the /E switch, or you have left a space between the / and the *E*. Edit and save your CONFIG.SYS file, and restart MS-DOS.

`Memory allocation error`
`Cannot load COMMAND, system halted`

ERROR: A program destroys the area where MS-DOS keeps track of in-use and available memory. You must restart MS-DOS.

If this error occurs again with the same program, the program has a flaw. Use a backup copy of the program. If the problem persists, contact the dealer or program manufacturer.

`Missing operating system`

ERROR (start-up): The MS-DOS hard disk partition entry is marked as "bootable" (able to start MS-DOS), but the MS-DOS partition does not have a copy of MS-DOS on it. MS-DOS does not boot.

Start MS-DOS from a floppy disk. If you have existing files on the hard disk, back up the files. Issue FORMAT /S to put a copy of the operating system on the hard disk. If necessary, restore the files that you backed up.

`No free file handles`
`Cannot start COMMAND, exiting`

ERROR: MS-DOS cannot load an additional copy of COMMAND.COM because no file handles (FILES=) are available.

Edit the CONFIG.SYS file on your start-up disk to increase the number of file handles (using the FILES command) by five. Restart MS-DOS and try the command again.

`Non-System disk or disk error`
`Replace and press any key when ready`

ERROR (start-up): Your floppy disk or hard disk does not contain MS-DOS, or a read error occurs when you start the system. MS-DOS does not boot.

If you are using a floppy disk system, put a bootable floppy disk in drive A and press a key.

The most frequent cause of this message on hard disk systems is leaving a nonbootable floppy disk in disk drive A with the door closed. Open the door to disk drive A and press a key. MS-DOS boots from the hard disk.

Not enough memory

ERROR: The computer does not have enough free RAM memory to execute the program or command.

If you loaded a resident program such as PRINT, GRAPHICS, SideKick, or ProKey, restart MS-DOS and try the command again before loading any resident program. If this method fails, remove any unneeded device driver or RAM-disk software from the CONFIG.SYS file and restart MS-DOS again. If this option fails also, your computer does not have enough memory to run this command. You must increase your RAM memory.

Out of environment space

WARNING: MS-DOS is unable to add to the environment any more strings from the SET command. The environment cannot be expanded without setting an environment size in CONFIG.SYS. (See **COMSPEC** and **SHELL**.)

This error occurs when you load a resident program, such as MODE, PRINT, GRAPHICS, or MIRROR. Refer to the SHELL command for information about expanding the default space for the environment using the /E switch with COMMAND.COM.

Packed file is corrupt

This error can result from two different errors. First, a program file may have become damaged due to a system failure, an improper program exit, or other system problem. Second, the program you are trying to run is not completely compatible with the way both DOS 5.0 and DOS 6.0 handle how programs load into conventional memory.

If you receive this error and know your file is intact and complete, your program may be one of those that DOS 5 and 6 need help to run. (See **LOADFIX** and **SETVER** for additional help.)

`Parameter format not correct - parm`

ERROR: You entered a parameter using an incorrect form. You may have forgotten to place a slash (/) in front of a switch or a colon for the drive designation.

`Path not found`

ERROR: A file or directory path you named does not exist.

You may have misspelled the file name or directory name or omitted a path character (\) between directory names or between the final directory name and file name. Another possibility is that the file or directory does not exist where you specified. Check these possibilities and try again.

`Path too long`

ERROR: You specified a path name that exceeds the 63-character limit of MS-DOS.

Either the name is too long, or you omitted a space between file names. Check the command line. If the phrasing is correct, you must change to a directory that is closer to the file you want and try the command again.

`Program too big to fit in memory`

ERROR: The computer does not have enough memory to load the program or command you invoked.

If you have any resident programs loaded (such as PRINT, GRAPHICS, or SideKick), restart MS-DOS and try the command again without loading the resident programs. If this message appears again, reduce the number of buffers (BUFFERS=) in the CONFIG.SYS file, eliminate unneeded device drivers or RAM-disk software, and restart MS-DOS again. If these actions do not solve the problem, your computer does not have enough RAM memory for the program or command. You must increase the amount of RAM memory in your computer to run this command.

Required parameter missing

ERROR: You did not specify a necessary parameter. Check the syntax to see how many parameters are required.

Sharing violation

WARNING: With the file-sharing program (SHARE.EXE) loaded, you or one of your programs attempts to access a file by using a sharing mode not allowed at this time. Another program or computer has temporary control over the file.

You will see the message Abort, Retry, Ignore. Press R for Retry several times. If the problem persists, press A for Abort. If you abort, however, you lose any data that the program is currently manipulating.

Syntax error

ERROR: You phrased a command improperly by omitting needed information; giving extraneous information; putting an extra space in a file name or path name; or using an incorrect switch. Check the command line for these possibilities and try the command again.

Too many block devices

WARNING (start-up): Your CONFIG.SYS file has too many DEVICE directives. MS-DOS continues to start but does not install any additional device drivers.

MS-DOS can handle only 26 block devices. Remove any unnecessary DEVICE directives in your CONFIG.SYS file and restart MS-DOS.

Too many parameters - *parms*

ERROR: You have given too many parameters in a command. Check to see if you put an extra space in

the command or forgot to place a slash (/) in front
of a switch.

`Top level process aborted, cannot continue`

ERROR (start-up): COMMAND.COM or another MS-
DOS command detects a disk error, and you choose
the A (abort) option. MS-DOS cannot finish starting
itself, and the system halts.

Try to start MS-DOS again. If the error recurs, use
a floppy disk (if starting from the hard disk) or a
different floppy disk (if starting from floppy disks)
to start MS-DOS. After it has started, use the SYS
command to put another copy of the operating
system on the disk, and copy COMMAND.COM to
the disk. If MS-DOS reports an error during the
copying, the hard disk or floppy disk is bad. Either
reformat or retire the floppy disk, or back up and
reformat the hard disk.

`Unable to create directory`

ERROR: Either you or a program attempts to create
a directory, and one of the following occurs:

- A directory by the same name already exists.

- A file by the same name already exists.

- You are adding a directory to the root
  directory, and the root directory is full.

- The directory name has illegal characters or
  is a device name.

Run the DIR command on the disk. Make sure that
no file or directory already exists with the same
name. If adding the directory to the root directory,
remove or move (copy, then erase) any unneeded
files or directives. Check the spelling of the directory and ensure that the command is properly
phrased.

`Unrecognized command in CONFIG.SYS`

WARNING (start-up): MS-DOS detects an improperly
phrased directive in CONFIG.SYS. The directive is

ignored, and MS-DOS continues to start; but MS-DOS does not indicate the incorrect line.

Examine the CONFIG.SYS file, looking for improperly phrased or incorrect directives. Edit the line, save the file, and restart MS-DOS.

MS-DOS Device Error Messages

When MS-DOS detects an error while reading or writing to disk drives or other devices, one of the following messages appears:

    type error reading device

    type error writing device

Type is the type of error, and *device* is the device at fault. If the device is a floppy disk drive, do not remove the floppy disk from the drive. Refer to this section which lists the types of error messages that may appear, and describes possible causes and corrective actions.

Bad call format

A device driver is given a requested header with an incorrect length. The problem is with the applications software making the call.

Bad command

The device driver issues an invalid or unsupported command to the device. The problem may be with the device driver software or with other software trying to use the device driver.

Bad format call

The device driver at fault passes an incorrect header length to MS-DOS. If you wrote this device driver, you must rewrite it to correct the problem. For a purchased program, contact the dealer or publisher who sold you the driver.

Bad unit

An invalid subunit number is passed to the device driver. The problem may be with the device driver software or with other software trying to use the device driver. Contact the dealer who sold you the device driver.

Drive not ready

An error occurs while MS-DOS tries to read or write to the disk drive. For floppy disk drives, the drive door may be open, the disk may not be inserted, or the floppy disk may not be formatted. For hard disk drives, the drive may not be properly prepared, or you may have a hardware problem.

General failure

This message is a "catch all" error message not covered elsewhere. The error usually occurs when you use an unformatted floppy disk or hard disk, or when you leave the disk drive door open.

Lock violation

With the file-sharing program (SHARE.EXE) or network software loaded, one of your programs attempts to access a locked file. Your best choice is Retry. Then try Abort. If you choose Abort, however, you lose any data in memory.

No paper

The printer is either out of paper or not turned on.

Non-DOS disk

The FAT has invalid information. This floppy disk is unusable. You can Abort and run CHKDSK on the floppy disk to see whether any corrective action is possible. If CHKDSK fails, your other alternative is to reformat the floppy disk. Reformatting, however, destroys any remaining information on the floppy disk. If you use more than one operating system, the floppy disk has probably been formatted under the other operating system you are using and should not be reformatted.

Not ready

The device is not ready and cannot receive or transmit data. Check the connections, make sure that the power is on, and check to see whether the device is ready.

Read fault

MS-DOS is unable to read the data, usually from a hard disk or floppy disk. Check the disk drive doors and make sure the floppy disk is properly inserted.

Sector not found

The disk drive is unable to locate the sector on the floppy disk or hard disk platter. This error is usually the result of a defective spot on the disk or defective drive electronics. Some copy-protection schemes also use this method (a defective spot) to prevent unauthorized duplication of the floppy disk.

Seek

The disk drive cannot locate the proper track on the floppy disk or hard disk platter. This error is usually the result of a defective spot on the floppy disk or hard disk platter, an unformatted disk, or drive electronics problems.

Sharing violation

With the file-sharing program (SHARE.EXE) or network software loaded, your programs attempt to access a file by using a sharing mode not specified for that file. Your best response is Retry; if that response doesn't work, try Abort.

Write fault

MS-DOS cannot write the data to this device. Perhaps you inserted the floppy disk improperly, or you left the disk drive door open. Another possibility is an electronics failure in the floppy or hard disk drive. The most frequent cause is a bad spot on the floppy disk.

```
Write protect
The floppy disk is write-protected.
```

MS-DOS displays one of these error messages followed by the line:

```
    Abort, Retry, Ignore?
```

If you press A for Abort, MS-DOS ends the program that requested the read or write condition. Typing R for Retry causes MS-DOS to try the operation again. If you press I for Ignore, MS-DOS skips the operation, and the program continues. However, you may lose some data if you use Ignore.

The order of preference, unless stated differently under the message, is R, A, and I. Retry the operation at least twice. If the condition persists, you must decide whether to abort the program or ignore the error. If you ignore the error, you may lose data or freeze your system. If you abort, you lose data still being processed by the program and not yet written to the disk. Remember that I is the least desirable option and that you should only use A after Retry has failed at least two times.

INDEX